Pure Attraction

to
Most Reverend William J. Brennan
Shepherd and Scholar
Bishop Emeritus of Wagga Wagga
1984–2002

Pure Attraction

Fr Peter Murphy

GRACEWING

Originally published in 2008
by Connor Court Publishing Pty Ltd, Australia

This edition 2009

Gracewing
2 Southern Avenue
Leominster
Herefordshire HR6 0QF

ISBN 978 0 85244 539 6

Table of Contents

Introduction i

Chapter One: Being Connected 1

Chapter Two: Pursuit of Purity 13

Chapter Three: Power of Purity 25

Chapter Four: Game Plan 45

Chapter Five: Good Characters 55

Chapter Six: Fully Armed 71

Chapter Seven: Temptation and Sin 87

Chapter Eight: Purity and Perfection 107

INTRODUCTION

When we were young, our mother insisted that we should not use the word 'get.' 'It was vulgar and meaningless,' she would assert, 'besides, there are better words than get.' But times have changed, as time always does, indeed time is the measurement of change, and some words have so infiltrated the data base of our minds that I have opted to entitle this opening chapter 'Getting Connected' with that word 'get'.

We hear about people getting married or getting a Satellite dish and we know that they are connected. The former is a warm, personal connection while the latter is less romantic, yet hopefully interesting. In both cases the connections, much sought after, may not remain.

Over time the round dish pulling in a signal from some distant satellite may become less entertaining, or dare we say it, somewhat boring, not to mention expensive unlike EWTN [Eternal Word Television Network] which is free-to-air. In such cases the unhappy client will disconnect. Some Marriages may also disconnect by means of divorce for similar motives: less embracing, a tad boring and certainly expensive.

The first case is unfortunate; the latter tragic. All admit that divorce is far too common and it is always a tragedy. It is a failure of love and life. How can one avoid this calamity? Some may say: 'Don't get married!' Clearly a response of negativity and defeat. So let's be adventurous and ask ourselves another question: *Has marriage failed us today?* It used to be a grand institution that was able to weather the ups and downs, for better or worse, even until death. Yet that is not the case today. It would seem that the use-by-date on Marriage has expired. For many young people it is outdated and since it didn't work for their parents why should it work for them? After all, why bother putting in the hard yards when divorce is ever imminent?

Before we start playing the 'blame-game' and making Marriage the guilty partner, let us ask another question: *Is it Marriage that has failed us or have we failed Marriage?* I adamantly believe that Marriage is innocent; we are the guilty party. It is one thing to 'get married' or to commit your life to another, with or without the Lord; it is another reality altogether *how* Marriage works. Many Marriages and relationships don't work today because we don't know *how* to make them work. We need to reignite *The Art of Loving* in Marriage before it is too late.

By way of example, let us use a car or vehicle to drive home this point. You are motivated to buy a car, perhaps for work reasons, or maybe for recreational outdoor activity on the weekend. Your reasoning or motivation is the impetus that determines *what* you buy; the type of car you purchase. If your reasoning says: 'I need a small, cheap-to-run car to drive into the city each day' — then that is *what* you buy.

Stop and take a breath. This car is *what* you own. The life of the car and its means of travel are now determined by another set of factors, that is, *how* well you care for it, *how* much effort you put into its maintenance. It is not a question of WHAT now but of HOW. If you don't service the vehicle and neglect to fill the engine with oil, to add some water to the radiator, or to check on the wear and tear of the tyres, then, the car may not last. In fact it will break down. Is the break-down the result of what was purchased? No, of course not. It failed because of your neglect.

In like manner, Marriage is what we get on the wedding day. How well the Marriage works is up to us. If it fails, don't blame Marriage but look at the effort, or rather lack of effort in maintaining a loving relationship. Perhaps we don't service our relationships as often as we should, or as often as they did in the past. Perhaps we have forgotten the art of HOW to love.

So before you 'Get Married' or get connected in other ways, perhaps to the consecrated state, or the Priesthood, ask yourself, 'Why am I doing this?' Then, ask yourself another question: 'How will I remain connected?' It is one thing to get connected, but it is another thing altogether *being connected*. One factor initiates the process, while another ensures its final outcome and success. Our aim in life is *to be* a success.

This book on the virtue of purity will help us to-get-connected, and for most of us to be successful so that we may one day enter unto eternal life.

CHAPTER ONE
BEING CONNECTED

The most important connections concern our existence: who we are and where we are going. We cannot know where we are going if we don't know where we have come from. What is the origin of the person? Have you ever pondered the existence of man at the dawn of a new day? Have you ever wondered about the meaning of life before an immense ocean?

But aren't we only clever monkeys? Are we not just another species, surely an advanced version in the evolutionary process, but an animal just the same? I agree that some people may act like animals, but that is not the issue at hand. Leaving aside the spurious reasoning for and against *Bible versus Evolution* argumentation, which could distract us from our purpose, please remember one fact. Concerning our origins and creation, the answer to the question is not an *either or* scenario, that is, a Bible Christian or a science scholar, but a *both and* answer. It is a win-win situation, God and science; the truths of divine Revelation and unbiased science.

Godly Connections

The first book of the Bible that discusses Creation is called Genesis. It was written in the Hebrew language and in a unique and symbolic manner that requires interpretation, says the *Catechism of the Catholic Church* (cf. CCC 111, 289). Christians have always believed in the historicity of Creation, Adam and

Eve's creation in grace, their test and subsequent original sin and fall (CCC 290-412). This is what happened. Divine Revelation tells us the *what* of creation and science can tell us *how* it developed. The two are not necessarily opposed — though some scientists are bent on formulating that hypothesis.

We humans are unique in the visible work of creation because we alone are created in the image and likeness of God: *"And God created man in his own image, in the image of God he created him; male and female he created them"* (Genesis 1:27). The word here for man is actually *ha-'adam* the name of the first human person, Adam. What a novelty! We are created in God's image. But God has no body, so how can we have his image? Although we depict God the Father as an old man, He is a spiritual Being. God is the Uncreated Pure Spirit who is all-powerful, eternal, infinite and all-knowing.

Only human persons are created in *imago Dei* [that is, Latin for *image of God*]. The image of God means that we possess, not by right but by God's goodness, a soul directly created by God. Persons are the summit of the visible work of creation. Yet in the order of nature, we are below the angels who belong to the unseen world. The angelic realm, the unseen world of innumerable spiritual creatures, was also created in God's image.

So the *imago Dei* directly refers to the creation of the human spiritual soul. It is the spiritual soul that reflects the image of God (CCC 1703). God willed, however, that unlike the angels we would be created as a body-soul composite. It is the person who reflects the image of God because the human being is the only bodily being with spiritual powers flowing from his immortal soul, powers that enable him: (1) to think, that is, to reason [which is what we are doing right now]; (2) and to choose, that is, free will. [You exercise your free will every time you turn a page of this book.]

Apart from being enshrined in Church teaching, this belief in the spiritual nature of the person spans most cultures and civilizations. Be it the Aborigines of the Outback or the

Egyptians during the era of the Pharaohs, one does not need to believe in God to be convinced of the spiritual nature of the human person. The famous Greek philosophers, Plato and Aristotle, four centuries before Christ, provided rational proof and argumentation to illustrate that humans are unique beings endowed with a spirit capable of knowing the truth and loving the good [cf. Plato, *Phaedo, Phaedrus;* Aristotle, *De Anima, Metaphysics*].

It is only in recent centuries that the folly of Marxism, clothed in materialism, has attempted to deny this fundamental truth of our existence. Lamentably, many today think that we are nothing more than clever animals, who were fortunate to have surpassed the other species on the evolutionary express-lane of progress. Documentaries, films, books, biology have relegated our spiritual capacities of reason to the function of the brain. The brain is an instrument of the mind, a term derived from the Latin word *mens*. The mind is a spiritual power that employs the brain, just as we use the mobile phone to communicate by SMS.

For that reason the Church initiated at the very beginning of the moral section [Part Three] of its Catechism a paragraph entitled *The Dignity of the Human Person* (CCC 1700) as a basic human principle. A principle is a fundamental rule or precept that governs activity. The most important principle for us is our dignity — that we were created in the image and likeness of God.

Why did God create us in this unique fashion? In terms reminiscent of the 'old catechism days' we are told that God created us with this spiritual soul and put us in the world so that we would know Him, love Him and serve Him and thus enter eternal life with Him in the next life (CCC 356, 1721). Thus, unlike the animals and plants of this world, our existence was willed by God from all eternity so that we after this life might be with God forever in Heaven: *"Before I formed you in the womb I knew you, and before you were born I consecrated you"* (Jeremiah 1:5).

Personal Connections

We have been called by God into existence. This calling is unique for each and every person—you did not just happen. And God does not create junk! It was not by accident that you came to be. God has willed your existence for a reason and a purpose; a glorious beatitude awaits you in the next life. "What no eye has seen, nor ear heard, nor the heart of man conceived, what God has prepared for those who love him" (1 Corinthians 2:9).

The basic meaning of vocation is being called. The word vocation comes from the Latin verb, *vocare:* meaning to call, to summon. And who is it who calls? God summons you unto Himself. When you arrive, God will then be 'all in all' in everlasting life (1 Corinthians 15:28).

Whatever our status may be, or destiny in life, we cannot fulfil our vocation alone. In the beginning, Adam is alone, being unlike other creatures, and unfulfilled. Who says so? God did. We were not created to be alone: *"it is not good that the man should be alone"* (Genesis 2:18).

If we were not created to be alone, then we are meant to be united to another. To be *united with* another means to be in communion with another. *The other*, by the way, is meant to be another person; we were created to love *persons*, not things or other creatures.

Remember in the first book of the Bible, God's holy Word, we read that Adam was the steward of all creation, the vast cosmos, for it was given to him to name the various creatures. Here we have some Bible code-language: to name means to have authority and power. Yet after naming all the creatures Adam still found that he was alone (Genesis 2:20).

Adam's solitude was resolved by God who created Eve from his side and ever since *"a man leaves his father and his mother and cleaves to his wife, and they become one flesh"* (Genesis 2:24). This communion of persons, the union of two-in-one-flesh, is a great mystery. In Genesis, there is no mention of male or female, of human sexuality, until Eve is created. By implication one may assert that sexuality is fitting and meaningful only when both sexes are present, male and female. In stark terms, Pope John Paul II in his talks on human sexuality, called the *Theology of the Body*, asserted that "masculinity and femininity" are "two ways of 'being a body,' being a person. So much for same-sex relationships!

The mutual sexes, both created in *imago Dei*, partake of equal dignity and complement each other by their differences. Each person is fulfilled by the other and attains perfection by giving of themselves to become two in one flesh, as bridegroom and bride.

At a deeper level, this nuptial union between the bridegroom and the bride in the primordial marriage covenant also reflects the Trinitarian love of God. The word *covenant* here, often misunderstood to mean *contract*, actually refers to a sacred bond established between God and His people. For further information on this theme refer to Scott Hahn and his book, *First Comes Love*, to piece together the bigger picture.

Our God is personal and triune. The Father loves the Son, and the Son loves the Father, and from their mutual giving of love comes forth the gift of life, the Holy Spirit. So the Trinity means that there are three-in-one Persons in God. God willed a similar design for us because we alone are created in His image. So in the Marriage covenant, husband loves wife, and the wife loves the husband, and from their mutual gift of love, comes forth, by divine decree, the gift of life, a child: three persons-in-one. It is precisely here that we locate a most sacred and important principle that governs the whole domain of human sexuality and inter-personal relationships.

This principle being a moral one provides clear boundaries concerning human activities. In recent years the Popes have expounded its significance in Church documents: Paul VI, *Humanae Vitae* 1968; John Paul II, *Familiaris Consortio* 1981. The principle asserts that the sexual act of spouses is one act comprised of two dimensions: *unitive* [mutual gift of love in marriage] and *procreative* [potential gift of life] (CCC 2363; CCC 496). The two sides of the one marriage act — gift of love and gift of life—cannot be separated. Think about a coin that consists of two sides: heads and tails. Neither side can be removed without destroying the coin. So also neither dimension can be removed from the sexual act without destroying its nature and meaning. Now, we still have some other connections to deliberate on.

Loving Connections

In Marriage, each person is called to be united with another person of the opposite sex. That is the *what* of their vocation. But *how* does it work? How did it work in the beginning? How did Adam and Eve bond to each other before sin entered the world? And are we meant to bond as they did? In what manner are we called to bond to another person? Remember, our vocation is to be united with another person—a communion of persons. Our first parents lived this communion to perfection before the Fall. But what was the nucleus of their covenantal commitment? Clearly love is a central ingredient. God has called us unto Himself and 'God is love' (1 John 4:8), so we too are called to love. Our vocation is that of love. But what is love?

I need to admit that we have a problem here with the English language. Some languages use different words for desire and love. In English, however, the word 'love' is employed for all affection and desire to such an extent that it has become commonplace. One sees stickers on cars that read: 'I love Swans' or 'I love Sydney'. When people state that they love God, they love mum and they love Sydney, though the verbal syntax remains constant—I love—the modality of affection does vary. It is okay to desire such things as vegemite on your toast in the morning or a Mars bar when you're hungry but you should not *love* them.

The word 'love' is thus over-utilized resulting in a significant loss of specificity. For that reason, among others, C.S. Lewis, a great Christian writer and literary scholar, wrote a classic book on love entitled *The Four Loves* in which he lucidly explains the four Greek words for love and their specific meaning. In more recent time, in 2005, Pope Benedict's Encyclical Letter: *God is Love*, sets forth a clear presentation of the diverse meanings of love.

So for us the word love is rather special and refined. It is best reserved to people. Deep within our hearts, God buried a desire for true love. We all want to be loved by another person and to love another. Yet how does one find this type of love? And then once achieved, how is it maintained? These questions are not readily answered in just a few words. What can be answered is the type of love required to love another and the type of love that the heart hungers to receive from another.

In 1995, the Church issued a document from the Pontifical Council for the Family entitled *The Truth and Meaning of Human Sexuality*. Like many other Church or Magisterial documents this one remains an unexplored jewel, a treatise on sexuality, much needed, yet often neglected — what a loss! At the outset of the text, when it discusses the reality of human love and the vocation of love, it mentions specifically, and repeatedly, the phrase 'self-giving love'.

The document refers to types of love such as love of pleasure and love of friends and then adds that the person is capable of a much higher love which is the love of persons for themselves. This love in Greek is termed *agape:* gift-love or charity. Drawn from God, this type of love is a generous one that desires the 'good' of another because she or he is recognised as worthy of being loved. Why is the other person worthy of being loved? Simply because they are made in the image of God. This is the love that engenders communion between persons as it considers the good of the other as his or her own good. This love is a self-giving love proper to the communion of persons where one learns the value and meaning of loving and of being loved. This is precisely the love of God that we need in Marriage.

Integrated Connections

There is an old adage that says: 'You cannot give what you have not got.' To bestow on another self-giving love, the lover must already possess it. Self-giving love of its very nature implies selfless love. Such a love is not innate; we are born not selfless but selfish. Yes, that gorgeous baby, with those big eyes and puffy cheeks, will have to be taught to share, to be kind, to be patient with others, and so on. There is no on-off switch for virtue; it comes with age, experience and much hard work. Furthermore, self-giving love is the fruit of personal internal effort coupled to God's power source called grace.

With respect to our personal effort, we ought not to forget that any effort will involve both body and soul. Self-giving love means giving of self and not being preoccupied with one's own wants, desires and longings. Such a state of mind and moral disposition implies a certain interior harmony, unity of life and peace of soul.

In the Catechism, in the article on the Sixth Commandment, immediately after the section: *"Male and Female He created them..."* we note a lengthy and detailed section entitled *"Vocation to Chastity"* that includes twenty-three paragraphs, CCC 2337-2359. It sets forth the Christian moral teaching on human sexuality. The importance and placement of this section must not be undervalued. Why has the Church given such importance to chastity? Why after the piece on our *'Vocation to Love'* do we have a section on *'Vocation to Chastity'*? It is about time we revisited this important and essential virtue. Today, many cannot spell the word 'chastity', much less know what it means!

At Mass, some years ago, on the feast of Saint Maria Goretti, a priest I know preached on why Maria was willing to die for her chastity, which in turn resulted in her martyrdom and sainthood. A teenage girl upon leaving the church turned to her mother and said: 'What is chastity?' She had never been taught about chastity in the Catholic High School, though she had received sex education. Years later, that girl fell into the pit of fornication and unmarried motherhood. God is merciful, though; since then, she has returned to the faith and is now happily married. Yet if she had been instructed in chastity during those teenage years, how different her life may have been. A stitch in time saves nine, as the saying goes. We need chastity because we need to avoid sin. Unlike good health, sickness is contagious - flues and colds are readily shared in most homes each winter. Likewise sin abounds among sinners for we have a propensity to sin as we do to become sick.

When did this all begin? After the Fall of our first parents, sin, suffering and death entered the world (cf., Romans 5:12). Constituent elements of our fallen nature are disordered drives and longings of the body and heart called concupiscence (CCC 1264). These drives concern our bodily pleasures: eating, drinking and sexual activity. *"For all that is in the world, the lust of the flesh and the lust of the eyes and the pride of life, is not of the Father but is of the world"* (1 John 2:16).

Inherent in our fallen nature are drives and urges needing to be controlled. If anyone attempts to deny the existence of original sin and its effects, then they are either not a parent or they have had nothing whatsoever to do with children. Just witness children at play to gauge how feelings and drives can be truly warped. The fickle and contrary moods of little children, bent on sheer self-gratification, will clearly illustrate the need for self-mastery. Anyone who has succeeded at sport, and Australians are proud of their sport, must admit that success comes only after much self-discipline.

Being born in the *imago Dei* we have free will. Therefore we are called to self-mastery, that is, to be masters of self, lest we be mastered by our passions and desires. Let me clarify at this stage, that we are not discussing the repression of natural drives. Irrespective of the opinions of some psychologists, unnatural repression is not the aim of chastity. Chastity is the liberation from slavery, not the enslavement of mental well-being. If it is deemed noble for an Olympic swimmer to practise self-mastery by abstaining from certain foods and enduring a daily programme of horrendous hours of physical exercise to obtain a gold medal, why is it not likewise noble for a Christian to abstain from certain pleasures to attain a crown of everlasting glory? Saint Paul in writing to the faithful at Thessalonika, had this to say concerning fornication - sexual activity outside of marriage. *"For this is the will of God, your sanctification, that you abstain from immorality, that each one of you know how to control his own body in holiness and honour, not in the passion of lust like heathens who do not know God"* (1 Thessalonians 4: 3-5).

Each one of us must learn - it does not come naturally - to control our own body not in a repressive manner but to give honour to God. Chastity is the virtue that enables us to control our urges and desires for sexual pleasure. A chaste person is not self-centred, nor is he or she a slave to the passions of the body, but able to relate well with others and to treat others with the tenderness and respect that is owed to them. Irrespective of your calling, that is, your Godly vocation, be it Marriage, the Priesthood or consecrated state, chastity is an essential component for success, happiness and harmony of life.

Another word for this harmony is called integration. If you turn again to the section on chastity in the *Catechism of the Catholic Church* (CCC 2337-2359) this word in its various forms appears numerous times. Integrity is derived from the word *integer*, meaning 'whole' or 'complete'. Thus, a person who lives the virtue of chastity has integrated their sexuality. An integrated lifestyle is one that is well-disciplined by virtuous effort, divine grace and good choices, that has ensured a unity and harmony between bodily and spiritual dimensions. One can never claim to have achieved perfect integration or self-mastery in this life, as we shall see in later chapters. The example of Solomon, the wisest of all men, who in his latter days had many wives and committed idolatry, is a stark reminder to us all of the subtlety of temptation and our proclivity to sin.

In concluding this chapter on connections, we now appreciate the fact that we need to make the right connections in life. Integrated connections provide interior harmony without which one cannot connect in a self-giving manner with another in true love. What we all seek, that is, within the depths of our soul, is a profound *connectedness* with another. To achieve that, we need to make good connections and making connections involves respecting moral principles.

CHAPTER TWO
PURSUIT OF PURITY

We have mentioned how important chastity is for sexual integration and attaining self-mastery. Without self-mastery we are unable to connect to others or be united with another and hence fulfil our God-given destiny, our vocation of self-giving love in the communion of persons.

Whatever our vocation in this life, single or married, it is only a prelude and preparation for eternal life. In the Catholic Catechism, Part Three, after being reminded of our origins, that we are created in the image and likeness of God, we read all about our vocation to beatitude and perfect happiness, that is, everlasting Heaven.

Beatitude of Purity

Every human heart desires happiness. God is the source of this desire and the only One who can fulfil it. For that reason Jesus, provided us with the Beatitudes. When was the last time you heard a homily on the Beatitudes? Do you at least know them? Please don't regard the Beatitudes as mere platitudes or pious invocations because they are divine blessings decreed by the Lord. For that reason the Church has always held them in high esteem. At the outset of her Catechism treatise on morality they feature as basic moral norms (cf. CCC 1716-1729).

In the past, Church Fathers and some Scholastic theologians gave much importance to the Beatitudes in their moral treatises. The great bishop of Hippo, Saint Augustine, attributed so much importance to the Beatitudes and the Sermon on the Mount that he wrote an entire book on them. Likewise, Saint Thomas Aquinas, in the Middle Ages, after having clarified the essential relationship between the moral law and virtue, devoted a lengthy section to the Beatitudes.

Some modern theologians too have developed their own theories to give a foundation to Catholic morality. American theologian, Germain Grisez, speaks of eight modes of responsibility, which assert the existence of moral norms based upon human reason. Each particular mode or norm results in a certain fulfilment that is not dissimilar to the blessings of the eight Beatitudes.

One of these Beatitudes involves chastity and integration: "Blessed are the pure of heart for they shall see God" (Matthew 5:8). This sixth beatitude, "Blessed are the pure of heart", is classified by Grisez as the sixth mode of Christian response. It is a virtuous disposition of single-minded devotion to God, in which one directs one's entire self to living faith, and purges anything that fails to meet this standard.

What are the implications of this beatitude: 'Blessed are the pure of heart'? Firstly, note that there are two parts to every beatitude. The first part refers to a particular moral quality, or mode of behaviour, and the second part concerns a reward. The reward of the sixth beatitude — as is the case in most of the others, except the first and last — is in the future tense 'for they *shall* see God.' So those faithful who have had pure hearts shall see God in the next life. It sounds fairly grim for the impure hearts, doesn't it?! Perhaps we need to examine in depth what a pure heart entails and the meaning of purity.

What is Purity?

Any study treating with purity is bound to require many distinctions — and so it should. Abstract terms are hard to handle. That is, some words are difficult to conceptualize. Take, for example, these terms: liberality, humility and truthfulness. Notably worthy terms and virtues, no doubt, often sought after, yet rarely acquired. One can readily posit purity at the end of this list so as to form a balanced quartet, but that will hardly assist us in our endeavours.

What does purity actually mean? What does the average person think? Admittedly the notion of purity conjures up a variety of images and thoughts. For some, the word itself might refer to the spray called *'Pure & Simple'*; for others, it may imply a cleansing or purifying process, as is the case with minerals, such as gold.

But let us not be so profane; after all, we are attempting to discuss our sexuality. Surely a reference to purity ought to refer to persons. In this context, dare I suppose that we could attribute purity to those celestial beings, much at work—the angelic spirits—and much ignored, if not denied by some misguided souls. Clearly angels are pure beings, that is, they were created pure, as distinct from God, the Uncreated Pure Being.

The primordial root of purity is holiness. To claim that purity is a positive affirmation of sexuality compatible with holiness, is a reasonable proposition and not an anomalous conjecture unless, of course, one's concept of purity is likened to prudery. Prudery, as an attitude, is borne from the mistaken notion that sex is something dirty, unholy and needing to be shunned. As such it fails to understand purity. The sexual act, in this framework, is either feared because it robs us of our dominion or despised because it seems gross, empty, devoid of goodness and possessing only a functionary value. Prudery belonged to the Victorian era, a forgotten time and somewhat incomprehensible in our promiscuous age.

With what can purity be likened? A newborn child is surely worthy of the term pure. The innocence of new life, unspoilt and spotless, portrays purity. Or so it would seem. But do we call a child pure because it is uncontaminated? Is this the purity that concerns us? Though cleanliness is next to godliness, as the axiom goes, our thematic term still requires refinement. Our aim is to pursue purity beyond any simplistic and obtuse meaning so as to locate its essence in the realm of morality. Thus, from the outset, let us state that the parameters of our discussion are restricted to the domain of moral purity as opposed to physical purity.

Collapsing under moral decay, our present world *seems* unable to grasp the true meaning of purity. There exists today an inversion of order that tends to glorify the body at the expense of the person. One could say that permissive sex has divorced the body from the soul, from the person, which in turn cannot but lead to the fragmentation and defilement of man. When we desire the experience gained from parts of the body at the expense of the person, as such, then we have descended to the domain of the beasts. Only united to right reason can sexual activity be understood in its true domain.

Purity among the Ancients

Among the ancient Greek and Latin writers, the notion of purity implied chastity or sexual continence. Chastity was held in high esteem, though only within the context of religious ceremonies or motivation. Only those deemed worthy to approach the gods practised chastity. Considered in Greek mythology as the perfect sacrifice, young pure virgins were of exceptional efficacy in obtaining 'heavenly' favours. Among the Greek Philosophers, even Plato manifested his approval of chastity, that is, of a continence that originates in the soul.

Closer to the birth of Our Saviour, we find Plutarch, a Greek scholar, speaking about the importance of temperance and virginity of the soul. But perhaps the priestesses of the cult of Vesta in Rome are the best examples of 'chastity'. These virgins chosen by Roman law had to tend to the sacred fire of the Roman Empire—like the eternal flame—which demanded complete sexual abstinence. The cultic belief was that while the fire burned, the Empire continued to flourish. Beautiful young women of Rome were carefully selected for this sacred purpose and any infringement of chastity received serious punishment. If caught, the unchaste virgin was buried alive and the unlucky offender was scourged to death. Rome took chastity seriously! I wonder if such deterrents would benefit some at Kings Cross, Sydney!

Purity and Israel

Any attempt to grasp the hidden meaning of purity ought to give due priority to the Word of God, for it is, after all, inspired by God Himself (cf. 2 Timothy 3:16). The meaning of purity gradually developed in the Bible. Initially one of external cleanliness involving very exact ceremonial practices of the Old Law, it rapidly grew to that of moral integrity and interior sanctity prescribed by the New Law of Christ.

The Jews of the Old Testament often associated purity with faithfulness to God. Not only individuals but also societies could be pure if they worshiped God and abided by His law. Purity was associated with fidelity to God and fidelity meant compliance with laws and norms of worship. Impurity, however, was likened to something profane, unholy, and devoid of God. In order to assure their fidelity, the Jews had set rituals concerning external cleanliness. Physical cleanliness connoted purity, yet was never identified with holiness. Why? Because God alone who is divine can be holy; a God of awe and mystery, distant from man, who must be feared and obeyed (cf. Isaiah 5:16).

Laws for external cleanliness, as well as sacrifices, became more numerous and exacting after the Golden Calf incident in Exodus (32:19-35). It is a classic story of rebellion. Though God could take the Israelites out of Egypt, He did not take Egypt out of His people. Four hundred years of pagan idolatry and hedonism is hard to wash away with one crossing of the Red Sea. As a punishment for their sin many were slaughtered, and for forty years they would wander aimlessly in the wilderness — until the older generation had died out. The rate of animal sacrifices was increased, in addition to the ceremonial and cleansing laws. Such laws greatly influenced the entire notion of purity among the Hebrew people.

The closer one came to God, the greater was the need for sexual purification. For example, three days before the promulgation of the law, sexual activity was forbidden to the Israelites (Exodus 19:15). As a norm, Levite priests who offered sacrifice were required to abstain sexually before ceremonies

(Leviticus 15:16, 22:4) and to ensure strict obedience, severe punishment was meted out to those who transgressed these laws (Leviticus 22:3-9). One was also considered unclean from sexual intercourse and menstruation (Leviticus 15:18); not to mention child-birth (Leviticus 12:8). There also existed numerous forms of impurity when one touched a corpse, or certain objects, some animals, or if one fraternized with unclean people such as lepers or infidels (Leviticus 5:3; 22:5).

Purification usually required, apart from prescribed cleansing and abstinence (Exodus 19:15), various ceremonies such as sacrificial offerings, often involving a sprinkling with blood, incense, ashes or herbs (Numbers 17:11). In contrast to the Jews, we Christians have it easy, so never let anyone complain about too many Church rules!

Purity in the New Covenant

With the incarnation of the eternal Son of God who took upon himself human flesh, the notion of purity was radically transformed. What was once external became internal, that which was physical was rendered spiritual. Our Lord as the new Adam offered himself as a victim on Calvary and invites us to participate in His own divinity as sons of God. This elevation or deification of our human nature resulted in a radical reform of the notion of holiness and, as a consequence, sanctification by means of interior purification.

Interior purity is a constant theme of Our Lord's teaching: "Nothing that finds its way into man from outside can make him unclean; what makes man unclean is what comes out of a man" (Mark 7:14-23). Christ's teaching is tantamount to an inversion of the established Jewish order. Defilement comes from within, not from without. The hypocritical Pharisees (John 9:40) who highly esteemed ritualistic purity failed to grasp this novel distinction. Even graphic rebukes by Our Lord, such as the following, failed to moderate their attitude: "Scour the inside of the cup and dish first, you blind Pharisee, so that the outside, too, may become clean" (Matthew 23:25). Only with time, and the coming of the Holy Spirit, would there be a complete appreciation of the new domain of purity.

In Christian terms, purity became an interior virtue, a personal norm (Ephesians 1:4) flowing from the heart, founded upon truth and faithfulness. A life of charity, of living love, according to the apostle Saint Paul, "is based on purity of heart, on a good conscience and a sincere faith" (1 Timothy 1:5). Such a love requires total consecration to God (cf. Matthew 22:37) and simplicity of life. It pertains to both the body and the spirit. Moreover it implies not mere abstinence from illicit pleasures but the positive dominion of the Holy Spirit.

Purity as a Virtue

Just as all beings tend towards their end, so we too as Christians, born of a living faith, are destined to our end: the beatific vision. In order that we, as wayfarers, might arrive there Our Lord commanded us to seek perfection: "You are to be perfect, as your heavenly Father is perfect" (Matthew 5:48).

The virtues are essential for our perfection. The word virtue is derived from the Latin word *virtus,* meaning strength or power. We become holy through good habits, that is, the practice of virtue. And in this manner we can boast that we no longer live, but Christ lives in us (Galatians 2:20). Our Lord commanded us to love: "Love the Lord your God with your whole heart..." (Mark 12:30). But how are we to put this generic precept into practice? What means are available that will enable us to love and practise virtue to such a degree?

For a soul to advance towards God in sanctity, it must be first illumined with grace and purified from all worldly affections. No one can see God, or even hear His voice unless he dies to self (Luke 9:23). Moreover, to receive these divine lights we need to become pure. The heart must be pure and its eyes clean and candid (1 John 2:16); otherwise it will not see God (Revelation 22:4). Obviously, the sixth beatitude: "Blessed are the pure of heart, for they shall see God" (Matthew 5:8) is the exhortation *par excellence* to the virtue of purity. Perhaps that is why purity is likened to the heart: be it hardened to grace or open to divine impulses. The term *heart* was often used in the Old Testament (Genesis 20:1; Psalms 23:4) in reference to holiness in the sight of God. Also, instead of *pure* being used in a generic sense, 'pure of heart' was chosen to emphasise that purity referred to the whole person, to every aspect that relates to man and was not to be considered only as religious or legal purity.

Such a state of purity can only be achieved through virtue. Exterior purity, for example, is acquired by the virtue of temperance, which regulates the bodily senses and passions, including chastity. It requires much discipline, self-control and mortification (1 Corinthians 9:27); whereas interior purity is attained through detachment, humility, justice, charity and peace (2 Timothy 2:22).

What is Virtue?

In simple terms, virtues are good habits. Habits are the result of repeated acts. When you go bush, and I mean bush, on some fire trail in the Kosciuszko National Park, or thereabouts, you carefully follow the trails, lest you become lost or bogged. What caused these trails? Well, apart from the big-time machinery of graders and bulldozers of days gone by, some are caused by constant traffic. Repeated tire tracks on soil will eventually result in trails or wheel ruts. Daily habits in like manner are caused by repeated actions.

Our normal routine consists of numerous habits: morning prayers, brushing our teeth, writing, driving the car and so on. When the habit is a morally good one — as distinct from an evil one such as a vice — then, it is a virtue. So virtues are a stable disposition to do good acts. When someone repeats a generous act often enough, it will endow him with the virtue of generosity. In turn, virtues enable one to act with ease, promptness and pleasure. Generous souls find it easier to give than a Mister Scrooge who is stingy and mean-hearted.

In recent years, the writings of some philosophers, theologians, and psychologists such as, Alasdair MacIntyre, Peter Geach, Ed Diener, Christopher Peterson, Servais Pinckaers and Romanus Cessario have put virtue back on the academic agenda as a key element of moral action. Virtue has become a popular academic theme in recent decades.

All virtues reside in the person's soul, or, to be more precise, in either one of the faculties of the soul, the intellect or the will. In addition, a Christian's soul is equipped with infused or supernatural virtues of which three are theological [CCC 1812-1817: faith, hope, love] and four moral [CCC 1805-1809: prudence, justice, fortitude, temperance]. Among the godly virtues faith is the foundation, upon which hope remains steadfast, inspiring us to perform works of charity, which is the greatest of them all: "So faith, hope, love abide, these three, but the greatest of these is love" (1 Corinthians 13:13).

The cardinal virtue of temperance links us to purity which resides in the will and governs our sensate desires for food, drink or sexual pleasure. With God's grace, which is called sanctifying or habitual grace (cf. CCC 2000), all the virtues are endowed with supernatural modality and operation. Conversely, when we turn from God and choose sin we lose both grace and the ease to practise virtue.

Gift of the Holy Spirit and Purity

The Holy Spirit is the divine Giver of all spiritual gifts. Saint Paul states: "And my speech and my preaching were not in the persuasive words of wisdom, but in the demonstration of the Spirit and of power, that your faith might rest, not on the wisdom of men, but on the power of God" (1 Cor. 2:4). There is only one Spirit who gives his different gifts for the welfare of the Church. But there are seven gifts (Is. 11:2-3) each corresponding to a particular virtue which it perfects and complements.

With the Gifts, we are more passive than active. For the entire mode of operation is not only supernatural in its object, like the virtues, but also in its manner. One can say, as Saint Teresa of Avila did once, that to practise virtue is to row, to use the Gifts is to sail. In this latter way one advances more rapidly and with less effort: in a truly supernatural fashion (1 Cors. 2:14). It may happen during a retreat or at a recollection day, when your mode of perception concerning a particular Church teaching suddenly changes. Sandy, a 16 year old, once told me that it was only after prayer before the Blessed Sacrament, and I mean real prayer, that she was able to grasp the importance of Confession. That is the Holy Spirit and his mode of action.

When we do something by means of the Gifts, we are acting rather from the divine reason than from the human reason, being moved by a better principle than is human reasoning so that we act far more promptly, far less laboriously, far more securely, and far more perfectly.

The virtue of faith is united to the Gift of Understanding so that God may purify, illuminate and make clearer the truths that we have assented to in faith. But how does faith make the heart pure? God illumines the soul with His divine power called grace. As the sun can radiate through a dirty window, God's infinite holiness can permeate the heart, rendering it more clean or pure, detaching it from all unhealthy wants and desires other than God Himself. As a consequence the soul is blessed with the ability to view divine realities.

I suppose that is the hidden meaning of what we read in Malachi 3:3: "He will sit as a refiner and purifier of silver." For some time I used to wonder why God would refer to Himself as a purifier of silver, until I discovered how a silversmith refines silver. A silversmith holds the piece of silver over the fire and lets it heat up. One needs to hold the silver in the middle of the fire where the flames are hottest so as to burn away all the impurities. But if the silver is left a moment too long in the flames it would be destroyed. The pertinent question is: "How does one know when the silver is fully refined?" When the silversmith can see his image in the silver! God is the Silversmith and we are the silver. Only when we reflect Him are we able to partake of eternal bliss. So, beforehand, we may have to be purged in Purgatory. For Heaven is the beatific vision where we see God and God's image is reflected in us.

So as to assist in this spiritual perfection, the Holy Spirit endows us *now* with certain insights. Hence the divine gift allied to the sixth beatitude is the gift of understanding which complements and perfects the virtue of faith, adding depth to mere knowledge or belief. In this manner through these intense and luminous realizations God purifies the soul: "By faith God has purified the hearts of the pagans" (Acts 15:9).

In summary, the beatitude: "Blessed are the pure of heart" establishes by divine mandate the virtue of purity as a universal Christian way. This way is supernaturally assisted with the inspiration of the Holy Spirit, in the form of the Gift of Understanding, and ordered to an object corresponding to the infused virtue of faith; so that as a result the soul is purified of every worldly attachment, made holier and drawn closer to its end, that is, "to see God."

CHAPTER THREE
POWER OF PURITY

Until now we have attempted to explain the importance of purity as a Christian norm. In order to sustain this belief, we hold that the sixth beatitude should be understood as a moral exhortation of the Lord to all Christians. As a directive, it achieves fruition within the context of moral action; hence we discussed the importance of virtue as an essential means to sanctity. Now we need to ask: What is the very essence of purity?

The meaning of purity has always baffled spiritual writers and moral theologians alike: it can be understood in such a diversity of forms, each in its own right offering rewarding and legitimate insights into its sublime beauty and transcendence.

Unique nature of sexual activity

It is impossible to appreciate the domain of purity without first considering the unique role of sexual activity. Among the activities and drives of the body, sex bears its own hallmark. At first glance, the astute scholar might claim that chastity belongs to the cardinal virtue of temperance which also moderates our bodily desires for food and drink. Is not purity simply the same thing, the moderation of sexual desires? Aren't all bodily pleasures much the same?

It is true that sex is one sensate physical activity of the body that grants pleasure. We also gain pleasure from eating our favourite meal or drinking that coke or beer when we are thirsty. It can be physically exhilarating. But when it is all said and done, the pleasure gained from eating passes quickly and rarely leaves any imprint — apart from the added calories! In like manner, the pleasure we gain from sleeping or listening to music is important and meaningful, yet it is devoid of true depth and lasting value.

Sex, however, is profound as an activity and lasting in personal values. It leaves an effect that transcends the physical domain and imprints itself on the very fibre of our soul, not to mention the very creation of another one. The unique domain of sexual activity is enhanced when it is compared to other sensate desires. Conversely the abuse of bodily pleasures cannot but add clarity to these subtle yet poignant distinctions. Let us take a closer look.

The immoderate desire of physical pleasure gained from food and drink is no doubt a sin. But how sinful is it? An obese boy who waddles up to the KFC counter for more of the same is a glutton because he lacks will-power over certain foods. On account of his weakness, he invokes sentiments of pity and compassion in the same manner as does the 'happy' drunk. Yet not so of the sexual deviant. One who pursues immoderate sexual pleasure defiles his spirit, as well as others'. Sexual perversion transcends the physiological domain and wounds the very essence of his being, in a manner totally unlike gluttony or drunkenness.

We all agree that both eating and drinking give physical pleasure. The reason for such pleasure lies in the maintenance of life. After all, if one fails to eat or drink one dies. So the purpose of these bodily activities is fulfilled by its objective end — nourishment. As such, it is a means to an end.

Let me explain. If the purpose of my being on the train is to arrive at the tennis tournament, then once I have arrived, the objective of travelling has been fulfilled. The train ceases to be important to me. The train is a means to the end - the courts. While at the tennis courts, I may feel hungry and decide to satisfy my bodily appetites with chips and a hearty meat-pie. If, while being captivated with the action on centre court, I give no attention to the process of eating, is there any sense of remorse? Have I committed some transgression? No, of course not. The purpose of eating is for nourishment, which, of itself, needs not our attention, especially when the tennis is exhilarating.

Sexual activity, on the other hand, has its own purpose, its own meaning and its own end. It would be morally perverse to engage in sexual activity devoid of attention or intention. The unique nature of sexual encounters warrants complete attention. Why? Sex is a holy mystery. Its mysterious nature is twofold. The first concerns the intimacy of the person and the second, the gift of life. The latter topic we shall reserve until another time. The former bears the quality of intimacy as it touches upon the very mystery of love and life. Each of us, each individual, male and female, bears within an intimate secret. Nature protects this intimate secret by means of shame because it is too private to reveal to one and all. When we engage in wilful sexual activity we invite another to partake of that secret, we unveil our most intimate self to another. We surrender our being as a gift to be given and a gift to be received.

Sex as a Mystery

We Christians want to protect this gift of self because we hold the person as precious and unique. Thus, we reserve sexual encounters until Marriage, lest there be some form of violation or betrayal. By the way, this explains the custom of the veil used in wedding ceremonies. The word nuptial is based on the Latin word *nuptus, nubere* meaning to veil. So at a Nuptial Wedding we veil the mystery which is not yet revealed.

It is for this reason that when people abuse themselves in a sexual manner, or use others for mere self-gratification, they sense within a perversion or defilement that wounds their very being. Unless they cease these actions, they will eventually *blind* themselves to the mystery and meaning of sex. In such cases love is then replaced by lust.

As a mystery, sexual encounters can be deceptive. When sexual pleasure is part of the package deal of self-giving love in Marriage it bears the hallmarks of true intimacy and centrality. The mutual exchange and surrender of self to the beloved occurs within the context of true tenderness and chastity. However, sex only possesses this tender, mysterious and intimate gift when exercised as the expression of something greater — namely, wedded love. As soon as sex is sought for its own sake, for pleasure alone, its qualities are reversed.

Instead a being a holy mystery to be encountered, it becomes an alluring pleasure to be satisfied and conquered. And, although, at the outset, it may bear a distinct quality of fascination and enchantment, such elements suddenly vanish, revealing an empty selfless void within. In search of compensation, some add zero to zero, by attempting to intensify the physical domain and only plummet their souls further into nothingness. The depth, the seriousness, the mystery disappear to make room for an intoxicating and befuddling charm devoid of meaning that becomes stale and sometimes perverse.

Remember, the mystery of sex is not seductive but sacred. It is for this reason that God has willed by divine Revelation and natural law that there be not just one but two commandments to protect it. The sixth and the ninth Commandments prohibit immoral sexual activity in thought, word and action. God does not want to spoil our fun or make life difficult. The Father is not a 'tyrant' bent on our misery.

On the contrary, God is our loving Father, who designed us and knows how frail we are since the Fall. We are weak and therefore in need of guidance and protection. A good father wants to protect his children from grave harm and warns them about the dangers of fire, gas, poison and so forth. Likewise, God in these two commandments is warning us as our heavenly Father not to misuse our sexual powers. Such powers are good and holy when used in accordance with His will and our vocation.

Sex and Marriage

Only within Marriage, sanctioned by God and sealed with an oath [sacramentum = oath] is one entitled to marital love, the right to be 'one body'. Therefore any attempt to justify sexual activity by a cheap counterfeit love is a lie. The language of true love, wedded love, is also the language of the body. According to John Paul II, the language of the body is a reality needing to be lived out in chastity. In this context, chastity is a mark of fidelity; for it serves love: I am keeping myself, my innocence, my wholeness in order to give you the total gift of myself.

For Christians God's Commandment: "Thou shalt not commit adultery" (Matthew 5:32) should suffice. We know that God is omniscient and loves us more than we love ourselves. Hence God could not ask of us anything contrary to true love—He knows what is best for us. Thus, so called trial marriages are empty lies for they lack fidelity, exclusivity, permanence and the love of Christ. Nature is quick to remind us of God's laws. Everyday life reveals the sorrow and frustration of unlawful sexual activity. Some are burdened with the memory of failure and disappointment that may plague them with sexual diseases or psychological baggage for the rest of their lives. Real love is not satisfied with a fraction, it claims the total person. Such a love is able to say no to one's feelings and urges, and yes to fidelity. The Church urges us, as does the Bible, to be pure and chaste. We all need to be chaste. Even married couples must practise chastity.

True love waits

Today tens of thousands of young people support each other in their commitment to be chaste by belonging to the international association called 'True Love Waits'. Just *google* the name to learn more. It is a Christian pro-chastity movement that calls young people to pledge themselves to be chaste until they marry. When one takes the Chastity Pledge, one receives a fidelity ring which one puts on one's wedding finger as a reminder of the promise he or she has made to God to remain a virgin until marrying. On the wedding day he or she then exchanges that ring for the wedding ring.

Some years ago, a priest was promoting *True Love Waits* at his youth group in preparation for a Commitment Ceremony on the following Sunday. After watching the video and listening to some testimonials he asked the youth before him how many would like to take the pledge. Eagerly all but two put up their hands. He then asked these two, a boy and girl who were in Year 11 and going out together, why they weren't keen and he replied: "We don't need any ceremony to be chaste!" Both were Catholics who went to Church and were well respected by the others. So the priest replied: "The pledge provides great support and encouragement - to know that you are not alone…"; the boy interrupted him and said: "We'll do it our way; okay." He certainly did do it *his* way. Within a year she was pregnant!

True Love Waits helps one to be faithful! But don't misunderstand me. Just because you haven't made a commitment doesn't mean that you'll fall by the wayside or conversely because you have done it that you'll remain on the 'straight and narrow' – whatever that actually means! *True Love Waits* can only help; it does not guarantee anything. Crutches help when the leg is broken, but they don't replace the legs. It is a firm commitment and God's grace that matters most. Also, I know of some very influential mums today who were once teenage mothers. At some stage they decided to turn their life around and to connect with God and do it His way. Remember the old saying: While there is life there is hope!

In order that sexual activity remains within the domain of Marriage we need to learn chastity. Chastity is that virtue that protects us as persons, our vocations and our sexuality. All people require this virtue for sanity and sanctity in their lives – its manner and mode of operation will vary, however, according to one's state in life. Now the question arises concerning the relationship between chastity and purity. If chastity is so important why are talking about purity? Why is this book entitled: *Pure Attraction*? To answer these questions we need to make a distinction.

Fundamental distinction: purity versus chastity

If we are called to chastity to safeguard our vocation to love is there any need to discuss purity? Or are the two terms synonymous? The issue at hand is whether there is any real distinction between purity and chastity. Any distinction, even a subtle one, hopefully will provide lucidity to our vocation to self-giving love.

In short, we are going to put some theological *spin* on our presentation. So be warned that the following material is heavy-duty and one should scale down their reading for maximum absorption rate. In car terminology change your gears to low ratio and into 4 wheel drive. If perhaps that is not possible then don't worry just skim over the next section. A dear friend of mine who read a manuscript of this text at the beach fell asleep in the following paragraphs and was consequently sunburnt. So be warned!

Firstly, let us define chastity so as to provide clear parameters for our discussion. A classic definition by Aquinas states that chastity is *the virtue which moderates the desire for sexual pleasure in accordance with right reason*. According to this statement, chastity has as its object sexual pleasure. As a moral virtue it controls sexual pleasure, according to right reason and not whims or feelings, as necessitated by one's vocation: be it single, married or the consecrated life.

Thus the virtue of chastity is a reasoned control over sexual desires. Interestingly, the Latin word for chastity: *castitas* denotes abstinence, a refraining from sexual pleasure. Often other diverse meanings are attributed to chastity such as continence, self-mastery or self-control. Do we just put purity in with the others? In order that we are able to answer this question, let us turn our attention back to the inspired Word of God for further insights.

In the New Testament, Saint Paul provides much insight. Scripture scholars remind us that in the early Church morals were drawn from the Pauline texts. But did Saint Paul ever distinguish between the two concepts: purity and chastity? Or was chastity for him a very generic term that even embraced purity?

A close analysis of certain texts indicates two levels of thought. So as to encourage a good moral life, Saint Paul provides his ecclesial brother Titus with a list of virtues. Most of the New Testament was written in Greek and the word he selected was *agnos*: "Therefore women" he said, "are to be sensible, chaste [*agnas*]..." (Titus 2:5). In other passages, *agnos* is also employed for chastity (cf. 1 Timothy 4:12; 5:2; 5:22). Yet in other passages of Scripture we note a divergence of terms. Saint Paul adopted a distinct Greek word *egkrateia* for the spiritual gift of chastity, or, dare we surmise, purity.

Also when he lists the nine fruits of the Holy Spirit in Galatians, the word for self-control is not *agnos* but *egkrateia*. "But the fruit of the Spirit is love, joy, peace, patience, kindness, goodness, faithfulness, gentleness, self-control [*egkrateia*]" (Galatians 5:22-23). In addition, in his first letter to the Church of Corinth, Saint Paul makes mention of the unmarried virgins and widows who are like him, single and consecrated to the Lord. Such individuals are not *agnos* but endowed with *egkrateia*. "But if they cannot exercise self-control (*egkrateuontai*) they should marry" (1 Corinthians 7:9). Here Paul is talking about those who have received a gift from God, that gift which enables one to remain chaste for the 'kingdom of heaven' (Matthew 19:12). It is for this reason he uses the specific word *egkrateia*.

Why employ a new word? What is behind Saint Paul's reasoning? *Egkrateia* unlike *agnos* [for chastity] implies a positive domination of the body, a self-control of the flesh for spiritual motives. It is within a spiritual context that we can cleave purity apart from chastity. It is here that a clear distinction begins to take shape.

A famous Greek Christian writer, Clement of Alexandria (150-212), commenting on Saint Paul, claimed that *egkrateia* is a virtue of the soul and not to be confused with self-control of the erotic pleasure, such as chastity. Such a virtue, he asserted, cannot be acquired except by means of God's grace.

More recently, Pope John Paul II, on 14 January 1981, in his series of talks on the *Theology of the Body* made mention of this unique term *egkrateia* and its close relationship with purity. It is closely allied, he said, to the power of divine grace and the domain of the Holy Spirit.

The spiritual gift of *egkrateia* is given to those who are consecrated to the Lord in body and soul. The consecrated state, in imitation of Christ or in spousal union to him, is, however, unique to the new and eternal covenant. Everyone agrees that chastity is a necessary property of virginity. But we should not go so far as to confuse it with the consecrated state.

Though we can claim that a chaste virgin is someone who has not engaged in sexual activity, this does not imply that the absence of sexual experience results in purity or the consecrated state. The absence of money does not cause in and of itself the noble virtue of generosity any more than the lack of imbibing alcohol fosters the virtue of sobriety.

So purity as distinct from chastity is a spiritually motivated domain. We have gleaned from the Bible the distinction that chastity concerns itself only with self-control of sexual pleasure, while purity implies a more personal spiritual gift. One manifestation of purity is the virginal state - being consecrated to the Lord. Consecrated virginity was appraised as a divine gift in the early Church. When early Christian writers spoke of consecrated virgins, *integrity* was the term they employed. This usage of the Latin word *integritas* was a synonym for purity.

Today in the Catechism of the Church that same word is employed in reference to chastity and our vocation. Let's examine some Church Fathers' views on this topic.

Integrated calling and purity

When we say the Church Fathers, we mean those great churchmen who wrote letters and documents in the first few centuries of the Church after the Apostles. Often these writers were bishops who were responsible for doctrine and discipline in the Church, as, for example, Saint Augustine. The title 'Church Father' includes also those writers before the seventh century who were esteemed by the Church for their orthodoxy, personal holiness and unique contribution.

One famous Church Father was Saint Ignatius, the Bishop of Antioch. Incidentally, Antioch was the ancient city where the followers of the Lord were first called Christians (cf. Acts 11:26). The Roman Emperor seeking to destroy the Church, arrested Saint Ignatius in the year 110 and marched him to Rome to be martyred. Along the way, he wrote seven letters to various Churches. Those letters, originally written in Greek, provide rare insights into the early Christian faith. At Smyrna, Saint Ignatius greeted some consecrated virgins who comprised an important dimension of that local Church. From the earliest times, we can note that the consecrated state was fostered and held in high esteem by the Christian community.

By the middle of the second century the practice of virginity was widely diffused. 'And many men and women', claims Saint Justin, a Christian Martyr, 'sixty and seventy years old, imbued from childhood with the teaching of Christ, kept their integrity.' It was 'a pearl of great price' much sought after and given only in prayer. Another writer, Origen claimed that, 'God will grant perfect purity in celibacy and chastity, which is a great gift - *donum Dei* - to those who ask for it in the intimacy of their heart with faith and continuous prayer.'

In 249, a Christian African, Saint Cyprian of Carthage, wrote about the consecrated state of virginity. He likened virginity to a vocation, a divine grace, whereby virgins become like angels since they are consecrated body and soul to Christ. In the fourth century, virginity was granted official recognition by means of a public perpetual vow. The popularity of the consecrated state caused some writers to disparage the dignity of matrimony. One can only surmise what these prelates might have said about our immoral permissive culture.

Saint Basil favoured the consecrated state as a most worthy vocation. Saint Gregory of Nyssa, being more platonic, promoted virginity as a means of liberating the spirit from the body. At Antioch, close to the end of the fourth century, Saint John Chrysostom, known for his clear teaching, praised matrimony and virginity in his work *On Virginity* against the attacks of Marcion, Valentinus, Mani and others, who were preaching either continence only, against marriage, or promoting only Marriage at the expense of virginity. Although he esteemed virginity as the more perfect way he does not dismiss Marriage as an unworthy state.

Among the ascetical writers of Egypt, Saint Athanasius emerged as a leading figure, whose writings spread far and wide. Athanasius, an outstanding bishop, who never failed to preach and suffer for the Catholic faith, was on many occasions banished for his orthodoxy by the civil authorities from his Diocese of Alexandria.

Saint Ambrose at Milan in Italy, whose very sister Marcellina took the veil one Christmas night from Pope Liberius, considered virginity as a Christian pathway upon which many should travel. Ambrose was renowned for his passionate love of virginity, which accounts for his writing so many works on the subject: *On Virgins, On Virginity, Institution of Virgins, Exhortation to Virgins.*

In book two of his work *On Virgins* he compares virgins to their model, *par excellence*, Mary, the Mother of God, and recalls how she was a virgin in her thoughts, words and deeds. Thus, virgins are called to be pure not only in their bodies 'but also in their words, manners and thoughts...'. Purity is meant to permeate one's entire life. Throughout his writings Ambrose repeatedly draws attention to the importance of purity of the senses. For instance, in his text *On Virginity* he claims that the windows of our soul, our eyes, are the means by which we either see the works of God, or we look at the impurities of the world. While commenting on the *Canticle of Canticles* (4:12) the

Bishop of Milan likens the virgin to a sealed fount. She is a closed garden and the door therein is the mouth. Not mere poetry my dear friends, for is not the mind betrayed by the mouth. Our words often reflect our thoughts, and language betrays that which lies within. Man's moral purity or impurity comes from the heart: "But the things which proceed out of the mouth, come forth from the heart, and those things defile man" (Matthew 15:18).

A wholesome threesome

We now know that God gives us the *gift* of holy purity in order that we may live in the Spirit and not in the flesh. But speaking of gifts, did you know that all good things come in threes? For God has left his 'thumbprint' on Creation. We believe that God is a triune God. The Trinity is three divine Persons. We human persons are comprised of body, soul and spirit. There are three degrees of time: past, present and future.

Also there are three spatial dimensions: width, depth and height. You may not be too keen to discuss your personal spatial dimensions! Yet there are three of them. While you are exploring other examples to our threesome theory, ask yourself: 'Whether purity exists in a threefold manner?'

According to Cornelius à Lapide the references to purity among the Fathers tend to indicate such a division. Father à Lapide S.J. (1566-1637) was a Belgian priest – and a Jesuit - who taught Sacred Scripture at Louvain and wrote an enormous ten volume Biblical commentary based on the Fathers of the Church. Some years ago in a Roman library, I examined these scholarly texts. I recall the size of these enormous and ancient books, or tomes – as they are termed – and thought to myself: 'What a shame that other people never see or read such wisdom – secrets from the past!' Anyway if we blow away the dust of the past centuries, we note that he divided the virtue of purity into these three categories: *puritas corporis* (purity of the body); *puritas mentis* (purity of the mind); *puritas cordis* (purity of the heart). So let us do likewise.

Purity of the body

According to Saint Paul we are all called to holiness by controlling our bodies in holiness and honour (1 Thessalonians 4:3-5). All Christians are called to practise the virtue of purity: be they married, virgins or celibates. At a bodily dimension this task will embrace the virtue of chastity which belongs to the cardinal virtue of temperance.

The Latin word *temperantia* is a translation of the Greek *sophrosyne* indicating the supremacy of reason over the body. In Saint Paul's letter to the Corinthians, he uses this very meaning: "But God has so adjusted [*temperavit*] the body..." (1 Corinthians 12:24) to signify that the unruly passions need to be controlled. In this sense chastity preserves and defends the inner order of man against the natural urge to love himself more than his Creator.

In short, chastity controls the passions and soothes the impulses of the body — whereas unchastity is a lack of self-control, by which man in a very decisive way loses possession of himself and flings reason away for the 'lust of the flesh'. By preserving and defending order in man himself, temperance creates the indispensable prerequisite for both the realization of actual good and the actual movement of man towards his goal. For by moderating the feelings and actions connected with the sexual values we serve the values of personal love. True chastity does not lead to disdain of the body or to disparagement of matrimony and the sexual life. Chastity is a liberating force that fosters true love.

During a conversation at the local Public High School about *True Love Waits*, to promote chastity among teens, a not so young teacher remarked "Catholics are known to be prudes!" Somewhat taken back by her quip remark, a catechist beside me retorted: "Better to be a prude than a pervert." Few today would associate themselves with the former term - much less know what it means - and too many are sadly associated with the latter. I personally dissociate myself from both.

In the front-line of pastoral ministry one readily encounters not prudery but the ugly and perverse. In some cases the perverse dimension dwells in homes. Yes, that's correct: perverse home life. Home is no longer a haven for some children. In some classrooms every second child comes from a broken home, where couples are separated, divorced or divorcing, and mum's boyfriend or dad's partner are taken for granted. In such families sexual abuse, especially of teenage girls, is not uncommon. In recent times, Fr. Chris Riley, has voiced similar sentiments regarding sexual abuse in the home. This is a situation that is rife and most tragic.

Apart from physical abuse, sexual abuse is epidemic in the media. Internet pornography is destroying the moral fibre of many lives. Once addiction is established the bondage is difficult to sever because of easy access to the network. Any decent person cannot but admit that we are fostering a perverse attitude of sexuality that parades men not as protectors of women but as predators. What should we do to change our present culture?

Firstly let's face the facts. Statistics on teenage promiscuity remain daunting as do the hard facts on sexually transmitted infections and teen abortions. Moral depravity is out of control. Over the years most of the proposals foisted upon the young by the 'experts' of sex education have failed. Be convinced that chastity and not protection is the only answer. Chastity needs to be rediscovered. It is the only solution to our present crisis. Our young people are able to be chaste and pure. It is not a mission impossible but a possible mission with God's grace. We should never doubt the effectiveness of God's power to make us chaste. Later we will elaborate on this topic when we discuss spiritual combat.

Although this dimension of purity concerns only the body, we should remember that it is interiorly motivated and directed towards greater holiness. It pertains not just to the young but to all people. Spouses are pure in their bodies when they observe the norms laid down regarding responsible procreation and practise conjugal chastity, not for feelings of guilt but because within their hearts they sense the very sacredness of sexuality and thus possess an attitude of reverence for their bodies.

Purity of the mind

"Whatever you do, work at it with your whole being. Do it for the Lord rather than for men" (Colossians 3:23). Blessed are the pure of mind, who are pure in their consciences; free from every sin, evil desire and from all immoral thoughts; even from duplicity and hypocrisy. Virgins, celibates and even married couples are called to purity of mind.

In defending the holiness of virginity against the Vestal Virgins (chaste Roman virgins) Saint Ambrose, Bishop of Milan, discloses the very essence of purity as integrity of the mind. Let us follow his reasoning. He firstly stressed the good qualities of virginity but insists that there is an essential difference between consecrated Virgins and Vestal Virgins; the latter being enforced by law, not perpetual, and rewarded with gifts and money. These virgins are not really chaste because their purity is not of morals but of years. Then he asks: 'What good is chastity if it's not pure and free from all stain? The Vestal Virgins' chastity is in vain because it is stained, it is lacking in faith.' True virginity consists in a pure mind imbued with a living faith. Are we not reminded here of the relationship between faith and the beatitude of purity: "Blessed are the pure of heart" (Mt 5:8)?

A virgin, Saint Ambrose claims, is a virgin not only in her body but also in her mind. Afterwards, to prove his point, he relates a story of a beautiful virgin at Antioch who was taken prisoner and forced to choose between her religion or chastity: 'Worship the gods or be sent to a whore house!' It is better, Ambrose claims, to lose one's physical virginity and remain a virgin in the heart than to lose one's faith. It is better to remain chaste in the heart to God than to man: since without faith there is no virginity.

In his book *On Virginity* he again refers to the Vestal Virgins and claims that they lack purity of mind. Then he decisively affirms that virginity of the body — we may here insert chastity — without faith is of little value since the merit of virginity lies not only in the body but in the heart. Only virgins possessing purity of faith become citizens of Heaven since they enter the closed citadel with the virtue of faith. In order to nail home his point, he adds: remember Saint Mary Magdalen; though she was the first witness to the Risen Lord on Easter Sunday, she was forbidden to touch Our Lord (cf. John 20:17). Why? Because she was weak in her faith, asserts Ambrose, and hence wanting in purity. Hence faith and purity possess primacy over chastity.

Also spouses are called to purify their thoughts in honour and holiness (1 Thessalonians 4:3-5), so that they maintain right order between passions and reason. For the passions must not dominate reason, insists Saint Augustine, Bishop of Hippo, because the spirit of the person should always rule the bodily appetites. It is not the passions, as such, that are evil since they are good because they encourage sexual relations which is a good in itself. Thus, concupiscence should be condemned, says Augustine, not because of sexual pleasure but because it is a disordered pleasure that leads to lust, a lack of temperance.

The passions can extinguish the infused and supernatural lights of understanding. Thus, we find intelligent men who are spiritually ignorant and blind to purity. Unbridled passions little by little corrupt understanding, first the heart then the body. Our Lord said to his apostles: "What I say to you is: anyone who looks lustfully at a woman has already committed adultery with her in his heart" (Mt 5:28).

Purity of the mind requires that we look not with the eyes of the mind but with the eyes of faith. Every Christian must make the effort to practise purity of the eyes because chastity depends on it. Chastity is all-embracing; it requires total dedication of thought, word and acts. The implication of such looks was even discussed at length by Pope John Paul II in his series of talks on the *Theology of the Body*. When we look in a lustful manner it can rupture the bond of fidelity, the conjugal bond of spousal love. And therefore spouses, even though they may be physically chaste, can be impure in their hearts and looks.

Purity of the heart

"With all watchfulness keep your heart because life comes out of it" (Proverbs 4:23). The pure of heart are purified of all earthly attachments and dwell among the angels since all their affections and love belong solely to God. Purity of heart consists in not being opposed to God's grace in any form. It means purified of all desires, irregular appetites, pleasures and comforts of the world which take root in our heart. "Create a clean heart in me, O God and renew a right Spirit within me" (Psalm 50:12).

True purity of the heart involves the body as much as the spirit. Saint Paul calls the human body a temple of the Holy Spirit. "Do you not know that your body is a temple of the Holy Spirit within you, which you have from God? You are not your own; you were bought with a price" (1 Corinthians 19:20). It is by means of sacramental Marriage that spousal love is caught up into divine love and enriched by Christ's redeeming power and the saving activity of the Church. Christ purifies human hearts rendering their love divine.

On the other hand, it is clearly obvious that consecrated virginity involves purity of the heart. During the ceremony of a consecrated religious, the 'bride of Christ' signs her vows or promises of consecration on the Altar in the Sanctuary of the Church. The Altar is chosen because it is a symbol of Christ, her bridegroom. In short, the fact of consecration to God transforms the person so that the heart once consecrated then claims spousal dominion over the body. It is no wonder then that Saint Augustine would state that: 'Virgins therefore are holy, not for their virginity of body—but because they are dedicated to God.' Consecrated virgins who freely belong to Christ are exclusively His and want to please Him in everything: body and soul.

Some years ago, I was a part-time chaplain to an AIDS Hospice for women in Rome. On Sundays I would offer Mass in a small chapel for those who were able to come and their families who were visiting. This home for the dying was entrusted to the Missionaries of Charity, Blessed Mother Teresa's religious order. After one Sunday morning Mass, I was introduced to a gorgeous brunet, a nineteen year old, whose name was Amanda. Looking into her chestnut eyes, I smiled and said: "Did you know that Amanda is a Latin verb meaning – she who is needing to be loved." She made light of the comment and then disappeared among the others who were milling around. Later, over a cuppa, I asked the Sisters whether Amanda often visited, presuming that she was a guest of the girls. One Indian Sister replied: "O no Father, Amanda has just arrived, she too has AIDS, but in the early stages. Amanda comes from Eastern Europe, was into drugs and other things ... so she is here now." Sometimes the 'other things' meant prostitution to support the drug habit.

Some weeks passed before I met up with Amanda again. On this occasion, after some beating around the bush, she told me her story. Her life had been one of much physical and psychological abuse – she felt very ugly and dirty on the inside. She had never known the beauty of chastity, or purity of the mind. When she had finished, I said: "I want to make you as beautiful on the inside as you are on the outside." She replied: "How's that?" "You lack," I said, "true person-to-person love. Amanda who is deserving of love needs to find the source of all love, the personal love of Christ. You have been misusing your body at the expense of your soul. He died for your soul and body. Don't deprive Him of what is left. Open your heart so that she who needs love finds true Love." I heard her Confession, absolved her and then later had the joy of administering Holy Communion: what divine intimacy in a human heart! When Amanda died she found true love forever.

Today also purity of soul can provide tremendous consolation for those who have lost their virginity and want to come home to God. At a Sydney youth forum some years ago, Joanne, a twenty-three-year-old blonde, explained to a packed auditorium the meaning of purity of heart. She said: "I was seventeen when I became sexually active. At the start I could pick and choose which boys I wanted and for how long. It made me feel special and important. After a while though, I realised that some men just didn't respect me, especially in the morning.

Often I would lie awake at night feeling so empty. I had some good relationships that were special, some even lasted for about a year. But in nearly all of them I felt used, that I had to perform for them so that they would be nice to me. Somehow I came to realise that it was not me they wanted but my body and good looks. Soon after, a friend of mine became a Christian and she introduced me to her new friends. But I felt that my lifestyle had gone too far and that I had been too bad to ever change.

Then I had an experience that changed my life. It was at a Summer Camp that I mustered up the courage to go to Confession and found the merciful love of Jesus. He healed my soul and the priest taught me how to begin again by means of *Secondary Virginity*. It is when you consecrate your heart to God after you have lost your physical virginity. By that consecration you begin anew and promise to be true to Him in body and soul. It worked for me and now I am happily married with three children."

In summary, we can now claim that purity is altogether different to chastity. It has primacy over chastity. For if one is pure, one is necessarily chaste, but the opposite is not always true. For example, athletes who are constrained to be chaste for reasons of their career would belong to this category. Also a chaste virgin can be impure—in words, desires and thoughts—while maintaining control over bodily sexuality.

So purity safeguards and directs chastity. On the other hand, we should not highlight purity and disdain chastity, for both virtues are closely allied. Purity, however, is that spiritual grace whose object is our entire sexuality and belongs to the supernatural realm. It is by divine grace that one is endowed with a positive affirmation of one's being, body and soul, as male or female. Thus, for that reason alone purity is united to faith.

CHAPTER FOUR
GAME PLAN

The preceding digression into the meaning of purity proved to be of great importance. If we want to live out our vocation to chastity faithfully and if we want to find true love and be loved, then our sexuality needs to be integrated from a spiritual domain. Chastity or self-control sought from a merely bodily perspective is inadequate for the communion of persons. Only purity, linked to faith, imbued with grace suffices. With these distinctions in mind, chastity now refers to spiritual chastity belonging to the 'pure of heart.'

We therefore find the definition of chastity in the document, *The Truth and Meaning of Human Sexuality*, more appropriate because it refers to chastity as a *spiritual power* that frees love from selfishness and aggression (no. 16). The power or grace, sometimes called *dynamis* in Greek, is actually dynamic in its ability to transform our fallen nature and ensure the true and successful integration of Christian sexuality. It is only in the Lord and with the Lord who makes the weak strong that we are able to be truly faithful.

Alienated Sexuality

What happens if we don't successfully integrate our sexuality? Let us remind ourselves that this is not an exam. There is no final exam to pass in sexual integration. Chastity, as the Catechism reminds us, is a life-long task, it is a struggle that will endure until the grave, as is the case with all virtues.

Just the same, there are periodic ups and downs in our life, when it will be more difficult to maintain a state of purity. Pre-pubescent children whose innocence has not been defiled, live in a pure world, as illustrated by their faces. The adolescence to adulthood years are more challenging since our body is developing, growing and most fertile. If during this stage spiritual chastity is not cultivated then lust, its opposing vice, can take root in the soul, causing great misfortune and unhappiness over the years. Lust is in direct opposition to purity and hence true love. When lust enters into its own domain and defiles the heart and soul then sexuality rather than being integrated becomes *disintegrated*.

What is disintegrated sexuality? In anthropological terminology it is when a person who is a subject is reduced to the level of an object. An object is a thing. We persons instead are subjects with rights who have an innate vocation to love. As a consequence, the dynamics of intrapersonal love are inverted resulting in a perversion of sexuality and a loss of personhood. Such an inversion causes a certain alienation instead of communion of persons.

In brief, the alienation is twofold. Firstly, in reducing the personal love for another to a sensate want of the 'other', the individual ceases to be a person and becomes an impersonal 'object' whose body is sought alone as the object of pleasure. I want not you but the pleasure that your body gives me. Secondly, as personal love is not sought from the other, one does not attain reciprocal personal love and remains, as a consequence, unlovable in oneself. Being unloved as a person, one becomes alienated from one's very self, and as a result seeks sexual gratification for one's own body. Hence the numerous sex shops for those assailed by lust.

It is also interesting to note that alienation results in dichotomous language. Lust divides the individual's personhood of body and soul into two distinct realities. 'I seek sexual pleasure from *my body*.' The body, rather than being who I am, becomes a part of a whole, a distinct entity, owned and possessed by the individual. In this context, the body is used for enjoyment and gratification. Since the body is not meant to be an object and is thus misused, any *use* of this kind can rapidly become a form of abuse. Hence the perverse association between lust and violence. This may explain, in part, why our sex-besotted age is suffering from an unhealthy interest in body-piercing and perverse body-mutilation. Not an uncommon reality also of the age of Manichaeism, in which Saint Augustine lived. We humans just don't learn, do we!

Game Plan Rules

So it's about time we laid down some boundary lines. We all agree that any good game consists of set rules. What makes a good game? A good game requires these elements: the rules are kept; the referee or umpire is impartial; and the players do their very best. We are in a certain sense playing the game of life. The rules are the commandments, the Church is the referee constantly reminding us of the rules and at times admonishing us for extreme tendencies. All that is required of us is that we do our very best. That means in moral terms practising the virtues, in particular, chastity.

In order that we may be assisted in the practice of the virtues, let us now unpack these following tactics. Apart from the effort involved in any game, there should exist — if we want to win — certain practical game plans. Before the event, those well-versed in all aspects of the game will think up some manoeuvres based on experience, expertise, knowledge and skill, that will ensure success. And if we don't win, at least it makes the game more interesting.

The following are the three game tactics for the integration of sexuality:

* Know yourself: male and female.
* Be not deceived.
* Avoid all temptations.

We shall devote this and the next three chapters to these three tactics. After all, we want to be well-prepared in this life so as to win eternal life.

Know Yourself: Sexuality has a Purpose

God created man and woman in His own image and likeness. Calling him to existence through love, He called him at the same time *for* love. God being love itself, having given the human race existence, inscribed upon the humanity of man and woman the vocation of love and communion. As love is therefore the fundamental and innate vocation of every human being, it must be a form of love that encompasses the body and soul. We must be able to fulfil our vocation of love as incarnate spirits.

A man and a woman love in an incarnate manner as husband and wife in Marriage. Married love is unique whereby the beloved belongs to the lover in an entirely exclusive manner and involves a perpetual surrender and sharing of their bodies and souls. The union of two beings occurs by means of mutual self-giving: "And they shall be two in one flesh" (1 Corinthians 6:16). In this context, then, sexuality is a mutual and complementary gift of self to the other.

Every person is sexual in as much as every person is either a man or a woman. What I mean when I say <u>is</u> sexual is that we do not <u>have</u> a sex like we have a Ford car or a pair of boots; for 'to have' indicates a relationship between a subject and an object. Our sex is intrinsically united to our being, our essence, and thus to our very existence: a sexless person does not exist.

Also God willed only two sexes: male and female. There are no sexless persons and everyone's sex is given to him or her, together with their life, as a unique gift. Nor does one choose his sex, just as he does not choose life; he simply receives it. For example, when God willed the existence of Saint Anne, the Virgin Mary's mother, and infused her immortal soul into her mother's body at the beginning of life, a woman was given existence, not a thing nor an accident. A woman who would change the course of history.

Our sexuality is also a gift. Even if parents are able to plan the sex of their child, we must realise that the child himself or herself is not able to participate in that decision which remains a gift. Man, called into existence by the creative act of God's will – with the help of his parents, who are 'collaborators of God's will in the work of creation' – has been given his life with a concrete aim. Called into existence by love he is to return to God through love. Human sexuality has an indispensable part to play in this love relationship, for everything a man does bears the stamp of his virility, everything a woman does bears the mark of her womanhood.

Sexual differences are complementary.

Sex as a bodily structure can only be explained in one unique manner, that is, by its service to life. Sex serves procreation. Without the sexual organs, man could not fulfil his splendid role as collaborator with God in the work of creation. The sexual act is procreative by its very nature and has God as its Author. Any attempt to break or pervert the union between this act and procreation is a serious sin.

As I have already noted, the sexual differences between man and woman are not decorative but functional; contrary to popular opinion. A woman runs in a different manner to man because her hips are so structured to be able to give birth. Her arms and elbows are shaped so as to allow her to cradle a child. The uterus is for the development of babies. The menstrual cycle is nature's way, month after month, of providing the necessary requirements in the likelihood of pregnancy: the cyclic changes encourage pregnancy; ovulation produces a potentially fertilizable egg, the breasts enlarge each month preparing to feed a future possible baby, and so on.

Such changes and developments are interior and thus

hidden within. In a similar way, woman is more interior and spiritual by nature. She reveals her interiority when she receives a man and manifests such receptivity in her ability to nurture and provide for the well-being of her own life and lives given to her.

A man's bodily organs and outlook are external and focused on otherness. He gives of himself in the act so as to bring forth new life. In turn, his psyche is geared for the sake of others and his primeval drive is to protect and provide for those of his own. I have met young fathers who were somewhat irresponsible and lazy until their first child was born. On the birthday of their child, they changed. In a short period of time they became more reliable, dedicated and caring — basic paternal instincts became manifest.

The value of human life, the dignity of a human being created in the image of God is beyond our complete comprehension. Once a person exists, their existence is forever: for, although they will die, their soul, being immortal, will continue to live forever; it can never be annihilated. We can say, therefore, that the sexual act which begets life carries with it grave responsibilities that are both maternal and paternal and endure forever.

The fact that one possesses mature and ready sexual organs is not in itself a criterion for action. For the realization of God's creative plan does not depend on biological readiness. The sexual act is not a physiological reaction as it is in the animal world, but should be the realization of a love so great as to become a reciprocal and irrevocable gift: a gift of oneself to another person. For man and woman are called from the beginning not only to exist side by side or together, but they are also called to exist mutually one for another in the covenant of Marriage.

Sexuality is more than genitality

The sexual act involves the woman's gift of herself to the man, his gift of himself to her. The obvious physical pleasure present in sexual intercourse manifests a far deeper spiritual and psychological reality. Whoever claims that sexual differences are merely anatomical and only for genital expression has missed the point.

Couples complement each other by means of mutual self-giving, the giving of self. We give of ourselves in diverse manners. Just as there are four points on a compass to tell us where we are, so too our masculinity or femininity exists in a fourfold manner:

1. physical
2. spiritual
3. psychological
4. emotional

Often the physical domain of our sexuality receives most of our attention, and yet it is the least important for mutual self-giving. In human activity all four facets are intertwined somewhat like strands that make up a rope. In sexual matters, however, the physical or emotional can dominate at the expense of the others causing a degradation of the person. At all times the spiritual domain, that includes the reason and the will — sometimes called the mind — must provide a leading role.

In the sexual act, the spirit, one's spiritual awareness, is exposed, as on no other occasion, to the danger of being swamped by its physical desires. Thus, our spiritual awareness should be brought into action and held in a fashion correspondingly profound rather than being overridden by passion. When one is swept away, the order of values is often subverted. Furthermore the offender feels a sense of guilt afterwards that he has wantonly broken loose from the order established by God. The moment the sexual act is not viewed from within, in its divinely ordained function, but appears in its external aspect, stark physical brutality, the ugliness of some features make themselves felt.

Let us now acknowledge some characteristics proper to the sexes. Both men and women complement each other as "masculine" and "feminine" in an asymmetrical mode. What unites them are their unique traits. It is by mutual self-giving of what is proper to each of them that they are united and the *two become one flesh*. As sexual characteristics, however, will vary from individual to individual, we shall only attempt to highlight some general attributes of the two sexes.

A woman is slow to love, to give her heart to a man. Men, however, love in a sensual and quick manner. A man can love a part of a woman but a woman loves the whole of the man. A woman desires to share her whole emotional life in all its tenderness, depth and warmth with her man. In that regard, she wants to be affirmed by a man, to win his abiding presence. Being more interior she has a greater capacity to love, to give herself to another.

What is the nature of tenderness? It is an inner awareness of the state of another that surpasses mere compassion or empathy. Its emotional basis involves a closeness or awareness of the other's state that seeks to communicate itself by an outward look or gesture: by the touch of a hand or an embrace. At a psychological level it is awareness of the state of mind of another made manifest by simple words or general disposition. Tenderness seeks to convey itself in a personal, intimate and interior manner only to those who appreciate it. Being a vital component of the 'art of loving' it must be cultivated and sought after for it cannot exist without a refined inner self-control. In learning the discipline of self-control one needs to guard against actions which seek to exhibit sensual or sexual gratification by the male or emotive sentimentality by the female.

A man is afraid of dying but a woman is afraid of not loving. A woman wants to be loved so that she can show love. A man wants to love so that he can be loved. For that very reason she submits to him so as to capture his heart and become the centre of his life. As a result, she seeks, at a psychological level, to draw forth what is best in him, not just from his body but from all levels of his being. This explains why wives encourage their husbands in matters of work, hobbies or personal development. It is sometimes called 'nagging'!

Men are also capable of great love but in a different manner. He will focus all of his activity, all of his substance, all of his responsibility, all of his manhood on her. A man is fascinated with his woman, captivated by her mystery. It is for this reason he desires to protect and provide for her. As long as he is convinced of her affection he will give his utmost for her to the point of suffering and even death.

A few years ago, Brad Miner in the United States wrote a book entitled *The Compleat Gentleman* to help us rediscover true manhood. With subtle humour and erudite scholarship Milner explains the true qualities of masculinity as portrayed under the titles of knight, gentleman, warrior, lover and monk. It is crucial that the art of manly chivalry be not lost in our contemporary world — more so in those circles where manhood and, in particular, fatherhood, has been eclipsed by the feminist agenda.

Man's outlook, desires and interests are external and outward. Correspondingly he manifests psychic independence and naturally desires to be more involved in external affairs. Being more abstract, he is also largely verbal and conceptual about outside affairs. A man desires his intellect to govern his interior life, emotions and outlook so that he can achieve satisfactory outcomes.

This doesn't infer that he has no feelings but that they lie deep within and are therefore not so easily expressed or articulated. The art of communication requires much patience and some innovation.

A woman emotionally expects two things from a man: love, including emotional love, and support or affirmation of who she is. It is generally recognized that woman is by nature more sentimental or emotional and man more sensual. In women this sentimentality conceals her sensuality and seeks first emotional satisfaction, affection from men. She desires to feel that he loves her and that he takes pleasure in her: in all aspects of her being, from the most physical to the most spiritual. This explains why she takes so much care of her body.

In both sexes true total self-giving is an essential ingredient for a healthy Marriage. It involves daily sacrifice, unselfishness, sharing, complimenting, encouragement, comforting, tolerance and the God-given ability to forgive and forget. As there is much available reading on the difference between the sexes in any good bookshop, let us move on to the next relevant tactic in the game of life.

CHAPTER FIVE
GOOD CHARACTERS

Apart from the obvious differences between the sexes that will help us understand ourselves, we need to learn much about the way we think and act. The previous chapter on sexuality discussed who we are as sexual beings, male and female; now we need to analyse in depth the process of moral action.

This chapter is one of the most important in the book. The previous section, for example, dealt with objective matters largely beyond our ability to change. In the following pages, however, we shall put down some very practical and personal suggestions concerning moral choices.

Spiritual combat

Being a Christian today is challenging. In fact, it involves conflict because Christianity has always been a religion of warfare. Lest you become confused, we are not implying that being a Christian involves any holy crusades or ghastly jihads. Yet it will involve combat—a spiritual and moral combat. Any one of you who has been involved in the martial arts knows better than I how much rigorous training and dedication is involved in achieving high levels of success. Well, we also need to be trained in spiritual combat in order to achieve successful integration of our sexuality.

An initial stage of successful warfare involves full recognition of the powers of the enemy. Every sport has its opponents. In spiritual combat, the enemies are the world, the flesh, and the devil (1 John 2:16). The last one shall be discussed in the next chapter. Of the three, however, let us be very honest and admit that the most pernicious fiend is not Satan but man himself. For us, the enemy lies *within*. We are a weakened race, fallen after original sin. After the sin of Adam, humanity has collapsed under the power of its own perverse desires and weaknesses.

The unmortified desires of the body are the most devious enemy of our eternal salvation. In the beginning, before sin entered time, there was perfect harmony between body and soul, flesh and spirit. Such is not the case now. The wants of the flesh are so dominant and enduring that many of us collapse under their incessant demands. We know what we should do but seem incapable of doing it. In the words of Saint Paul: "For I do not do what I want, but I do the very thing that I hate. So then it is no longer I that do it, but sin which dwells within me" (Romans 6:15, 18). It is certain that without God's grace, His power, one is doomed to fail. This is the very issue that eventually converted the brilliant Philosopher and Orator, Augustine. With the realization that it was God's grace alone that empowers us to be chaste, he submitted to divine grace and surrendered his life to Christ.

Another fiend that causes turmoil is the world. As we cannot but breathe in the surrounding air so too we cannot but be influenced by the present world. The world is not evil, as such, but it has been perverted by evil hearts in its social, economic and political structures. Take, for example, the demented culture of death which is not satisfied with the murder of infants in the womb but is cultivating human life and death in our laboratories under the guise of research.

Ask yourself about the moral agenda of some of the television shows and their mega-stars. Our musicians and political leaders who advocate immoral relationships and decadent lifestyles possess vast influence over the population. Their influence is pervasive and unprecedented compared to other ages because of our advanced media technology.

So today Satan has acquired a new degree of domination

of the world that warrants our utmost vigilance. He incites with little provocation the tinder of weakened flesh into a consuming fire that readily possesses souls. So be not mistaken, if you travel the way of sinful choices that take root in your heart, chastity will be lost and your soul may be enslaved forever.

Repent and convert

We believe, as fallen creatures, that we need God's grace to survive. We need to be reborn and live — so that not I, but Christ will live in me. Such an admonition implies an awareness of our faults. Here we encounter problems. First, we find it hard to see our own failings, but we are all painfully aware of the faults of others: "Why do you see the speck that is in your brother's eye, but do not notice the log that is in your own eye?" (Matthew 7:3). Second, we all differ, and hence our faults and flaws will differ from individual to individual.

It is a mistake in spirituality or even psychology to hold that we are identical as persons. As every snow-flake differs in shape, though they all look alike from a distance, so too no two souls are the same. That being the case, then, each person will tread *his or her own* specific path to holiness. On the other hand, human nature being constant, the issues and problems that do emerge, though they differ, remain much the same. In spiritual matters, many differences are rooted in our moral predispositions as well as the particular graces that God gives to each person.

Speaking of grace, here is a very important moral principle concerning spiritual power. *God's grace does not destroy or replace human nature; it works through and perfects our human nature.* This means that grace, God's power, is not an additional quality to our personal nature as a roof rack is an optional extra attached to the car. On the contrary, grace permeates who we are, warts and all, and elevates us as individuals from the natural domain unto the supernatural.

Our main aim is to die to sin, and achieve the perfections of charity. As individuals, how we attain that result will vary. At a human level, the same food affects different people in different ways. Some young people who possess high metabolisms can burn up the calories of a mud-cake in hours; others who perhaps are more sedentary types will be only adding fat globules to their waistline.

Grace, however, being divine, unlike food, is always beneficial and deifying to the soul. It transforms us as individuals in a most subtle and delicate manner. If the results are not forthcoming as you would have anticipated, the fault is yours, not God's. Change your spiritual frequency, as you would your radio, to tune into God's wavelength. God helps those who help themselves! So God want us to co-operate with him in the order of grace and the transformation of our lives. He expects us to do our bit, to pull our weight and make a genuine effort.

To explain how grace perfects us, we need to dissect the person. Remember we are composite beings — unlike angels or animals — comprised of a psychosomatic structure: a soul-body unit.

The psychosomatic structure of the person comprises personality and character:

> 1. Personality: temperament, physical structure,
> genetic make-up.
> 2. Moral Character: environment, education,
> personal effort.

Many psychologists and sociologists classify who we are as individuals according to two main factors: heredity and environment. Some personality traits are inherited from our parents. Apart from the shape of your nose and the colour of your eyes, there are gestures, modes of speech, mannerisms that are particular to you, that come from your parents. Much of your personality is hereditary and thus fixed to a certain degree. One domain that is inherited and often overlooked is your temperament, allied to the emotions. Sometimes people confuse feelings with morals. Our feelings or emotions can influence our morals; yet they remain distinct both in source and function.

Our moral outlook is more variable and consists of diverse elements: environment, education and effort. It comprises the set of habits (virtues or vices) cultivated by a person in accordance with his or her accepted principles and values. One key factor determining our morals is education. As humans we never stop learning. Initially our parents are the most formative educators in our lives. The key formative years are from birth to the maturation of character (usually between twenty-four to thirty). But we are never too old to learn!

During the early years, from infancy to the beginning of formal education and even beyond, the child will be greatly affected by such factors as nationality, religious training, parental discipline and instruction. Once the child begins a formal education, the school assumes a major role in the formation of character. Through adolescence the educational influence can usually be broken down into several categories: family, school, Church, and friends. Although the effects of these educative factors are not always immediately evident in the young, they leave impressions that form attitudes and value judgments that come into play when the individual person needs to make choices.

One notes that environment is used in the broadest manner; it includes home, family, neighbourhood, sport, Church, etc. The environmental factors are almost too numerous to mention, and they exert an especially strong influence on the individual during the formative years. The influence of example on children is too obvious to be denied. While the most forceful environmental influences are to be found in the lives of other human beings, such commonplace things as nutrition, climate, neighbours and home life also exert a subtle but definite influence. Here again, the effects are not immediately evident in a growing child, but environment during youth is responsible, to a large extent, for those attitudes and evaluations that are most deeply rooted in the personality.

Personal effort is by far the most important factor in the formation of character, and it is so potent an instrument that it can modify, correct, or nullify the effects of education and environment. By personal effort we mean especially the free choice whereby through the repetition of acts, certain habits are formed and developed until they become second nature.

Information and education influence us but do not constrain us. No matter what we may know or what truths we have rationally digested we still remain free to choose or reject this idea or mode of action or that behaviour. In other words, knowledge does not cause activity. Moral action is a result of the free will. To claim otherwise would be to accept blind determinism. Computers are determined, that is, they are fixed to operate in a given manner. Our personal choices in life, however, are the result of our personal free will. We are the masters of our own destiny. For that reason, we say that a convert is not so much taught but caught—and God is the divine Hunter!

Being masters of ourselves we are also responsible for the formation of character by reason of the fact that any acquired habit is ultimately rooted in a deliberate choice of action. In this sense we can say that, whereas temperament is to a large extent what our ancestors have made us, character is what we have made ourselves. In its moral aspect a character will be good or evil according to whether the habits that predominate in an individual are virtues or vices. As we already briefly discussed the seven virtues in chapter two, let's move on to the temperaments.

Types of Temperament

Our spontaneous reactions to stimuli are part of our individual personality. Each one of us behaves in a psychosomatic manner according to our temperament. Temperament governs our hormones, circulatory systems, external and internal senses and feelings that are stimulated by objects. Rooted in our physiological structure, temperament is something innate and hereditary; it is the natural inclination of the bodily structure.

People who are naturally easy-going and relaxed won't react to a said issue, while others who are more sensitive, in the same circumstances, are agitated and upset. The manner of reaction is spontaneous, through our temperament which is somewhat pre-determined. Our axiom *'grace does not destroy nature but perfects it'* has its most obvious application in the area of temperament.

Irrespective of our type of temperament, our moral character and the goodness of our lives is not pre-determined. A morally sound character, that is, an honest, kind and generous soul is not the result of instinct or heredity, but of a good home life, a sound education and/or much hard effort in the building up of virtues.

Nature or heredity can lean us *towards* morally good actions or morally bad actions—but that is about all. A hot-headed young man may be inclined to drive in a reckless manner instead of driving with care. He could blame some of his erratic driving on his temperament, being of a sanguine nature, but not his personal choice to exceed the speed limit. In other words, our temperament has not the finality of a death sentence about it; rather it is the challenging note of a bugle call to battle. Nature does give us a push, but the perfection of this or any other virtue is ours to attain by hard effort and God's grace.

On the whole, psychologists differ about the classification of temperament. Just 'Google' the word 'temperament' and you will see what I mean. To keep things simple, we shall explain temperament as the pattern of inclinations and reactions — sometimes called feelings — that proceed from our physiological make-up.

The original classification of the temperaments is based on the predominant physiological characteristics. No individual possesses a *pure* temperament, for we all have a mixed temperament. But one or another temperament will usually predominate. The emotions are psychosomatic reactions of the individual and hence closely related to temperament.

The idea of the four temperaments existed for over a millennium before the Middle Ages. It actually was Hippocrates who divided humanity into four basic temperaments, around the year 450 BC. Hippocrates saw the root of one's temperament as being derived from the humours dominant in the body: blood (sanguine), bile from the liver (choleric), phlegm (phlegmatic), and bile from the kidneys (melancholic).

The basic difference between each is the amount of time it takes one to react and the duration of the resultant reaction. The sanguine reaction will be quick to occur but brief in endurance; the phlegmatic's slow and brief; the choleric's quick and enduring; and the melancholic's slow and permanent.

So the four temperaments are:

> (1) sanguine,
>
> (2) melancholic,
>
> (3) choleric,
>
> (4) phlegmatic.

Sanguine Temperament

Today sanguine persons are called 'extroverts'. They are the 'happy-go-lucky' types in society who need the approval and attention of others. Such persons thrive in a group setting, for they seem to derive their energy from personal interaction. Because they are affable and friendly, theirs is perhaps the most attractive of temperaments, but, in grave situations, it can be problematic.

Often they possess a simple, childlike faith that appeals to others. They are likely to be faithful to any state of life they embrace, and, whether in married life or the monastery, are likely to have a pleasant bearing and take delight in the simple things of life. If they lack the depth and drive that some other temperaments possess, they are nonetheless spared the tumult and pain that is its invariable companion.

A sanguine temperament reacts rapidly and strongly to

stimulation or impression—their blood boils, so to speak—but the reaction is generally short lived. Once passed, the stimulation is quickly forgotten, evoking no new response. Hence they are easily excited and quick to anger. Italians can readily identify with this temperament.

Each temperament consists of positive and negative elements. The sanguine's good qualities are: affability and cheerfulness; kindness and generosity; sincerity and compassion for the sufferings of others. Although the emotion of anger can be fierce, all is soon forgotten. Such personalities attract others because of their kindness and lively enthusiasm. One can readily imagine Saint Philip Neri of Rome being of sanguine temperament.

Their viewpoint of life is serene and idealistic with abundant optimism. On account of their openness and friendly disposition they make friends easily. Generally they learn quickly, although often without much depth. Their memory dwells on pleasant things and events and their imagination is active and creative. Hence they often excel in music, art, practical skills and are well-endowed with common sense.

The sanguine soul has a tendency to seek not the truth but acceptance. When involved with a cause or controversial matter, he will bend with the group's tendencies. Spiritual growth, for the sanguine, will depend on strong support from sources other than himself.

At first glance, the sanguine individual appears to be the very friendly and the most at ease in social situations. Nonetheless, they remain blind to the effect their actions or decisions may have on others. Being superficial in their relationships, they seldom are the ones who can offer strength and support to others—they are unreliable, not through callousness, but through their lack of depth. They would not organize a pro-life meeting outside an abortion clinic, for example, but would go if others invited them.

The main flaws of the sanguine temperament are superficiality, inconstancy and sensuality. The first defect is primarily caused by a false perception of ideas and the creativity of their imagination. While they seem to grasp the issue at hand they often see it partially and superficially. As a consequence, they make rash judgments, claiming to know everything, and formulate false conclusions.

Sanguine persons react rapidly and can quickly pass from joy to sorrow. For that reason they are inconsistent. Being easily aroused they often succumb to temptations of the body. With genuine sorrow they will later repent. But they cannot be relied on to go the full distance when the going gets tough. This roller coaster of highs and lows can result in discouragement or indifference. Others regard them as unreliable in the performance of their duty. To offset such inconstancy, they need to submit to the authority of another and by means of obedience learn to complete what they have begun.

This temperament being the most susceptible to sensuality often falls victim to lust, obesity and drunkenness. Sanguine souls struggle with chastity. Even when the external sensual object of attraction is not actually present their active imagination is busy creating alluring images. Thus they need to cultivate the art of meditation to control their thought pattern. Avoidance of occasions of sin — a matter to be discussed later — is a must for survival, in addition to the works of mercy. By engaging them in good works, they have less opportunity to fall into vice.

Melancholic Temperament

The word melancholic is a strange term with Greek roots that refer to dark or black demeanour. Melancholics react poorly to stimuli and are difficult to excite. But once aroused their reaction is strong with lasting results and memories. Its tendencies remind me of some dogs which, when ill-treated over a long period, can become very savage to those individuals whom they never forget.

Such persons are often rather virtuous, being well-disposed to prayer, reflection and works of mercy. The Irish, in particular, the Irish monks, were classic melancholics. With reflective intellects they are good students and profound thinkers. It is an ideal temperament for a philosopher and those keen on prayer and the speculative sciences.

I once heard the melancholic described as the temperament that longs for Heaven so that life on this earth always will be a disappointment, and I believe that tag is apt. The depth and dedication of the melancholic will meet or exceed that of the choleric, but his natural caution and slowness to embrace new courses of action can leave him with a sense of having no way to channel his profound ideals.

The melancholic will base his action on concepts often so lofty that those of other temperaments will be beyond comprehending the motivation. The idealism of the melancholic, so centred in an awareness of divine power makes him the likely target for deception since, being focused on truth and honesty, it will not occur to him that others do not have similar ideals as himself.

The devout melancholic will be inclined to seek a high degree of virtue, because union with God will be an overwhelming focus, and it will indeed be God alone that he seeks to please. Even his frequent devotion to the service of others will be focused on ultimately pleasing God towards whom his devotion is passionate.

When they love, it is forever. Once they commit themselves, they remain loyal and faithful. It is for this reason that they find ingratitude and inconsistency very disagreeable. In some ways they are the exact opposite to the sanguine. If they enjoy good health then they are most reliable and dedicated to their work and lifestyle.

Such individuals need encouragement as we all do. In recent times, Pope Benedict wrote his second Encyclical (2007) on *hope* to bolster the hearts of many young people. Hope is the anticipation of expectations, the fulfilment of dreams; and the greatest source of hope is God. Melancholic souls need to trust more in God and not in themselves.

Choleric Temperament

Many of those venerated as the greatest saints were of either choleric or melancholic disposition. Not, of course, because those of any particular temperament are pre-disposed towards sanctity, but because their depth and intensity made them more likely to possess ardent zeal and enthusiasm.

Naturally, this proverbial two-edged sword also gives those with these temperaments the potential for a lengthy drop if they should fall! The choleric's strength is zeal, his weakness anger. How he channels his great personal conviction and power makes all the difference. His approach is never in half-measure, and what he embraces as most important in his life can make him the greatest of saints or the most graphic of sinners.

Since our profound choleric and melancholic friends often have temperaments which are respectively fire and ice, they are likely to 'leave their mark' on the world. But if the choleric can find his downfall in anger, the melancholic's Achilles' heel is sadness and despair. They are often inclined to exaggerate difficulties and problems and thus lose all hope. Being fearful and timid they lose confidence in themselves and others and exaggerate the unimportant matters at hand. In turn, they clam up like an oyster, not revealing their feelings and become prophets of doom and gloom. Once this stage has been reached, they may turn to drink and drugs in order to escape from their problems.

The cholerics are often called 'achievers.' Many a choleric has earned glory, but personal acclaim is never his sole concern. Nor is the influence of the choleric confined to the battlefield and Parliament! I believe that Saint Ignatius of Loyola, knight and mystic, was clearly a choleric. No one sought glory less, in fact, he thought himself to be the least of all. But his dedication was total, and, once he realised what the divine call was for his life and that of his soldiers, the Company of Jesus, known as the Jesuits, nothing could cause him to deviate from that goal. Thus, we must not view the choleric merely as the 'general.'

The same saint who was capable of enormous tenderness, and who'd bathe the wounds of the poor leper, was inclined towards tart reproaches to anyone who compromised the truths of the faith.

If a choleric 'goes astray' it will be from bitterness and anger, though his principles generally remain unshaken. He is apt to lose patience with those who lack his depth. Trust in divine providence is critical for the choleric but difficult to develop.

He is as likely to intimidate others as he is to inspire them. Their high energy output, sharp intellect, strong will and good powers of concentration can daunt the faint hearted. As soon as one task is complete they are engaged in another. Being filled with enthusiasm no job is left undone and no obstacle is too great for them. One readily associates these traits with the Germans or Swiss who pride themselves on punctuality, order and hard work.

On the down side, they do not tolerate fools and are prone to impatience and anger. However, once the task is completed they do not harbour bitterness but become tender and kind in disposition. One problematic flaw is pride and obstinacy that can turn to cruelty. Ambition and vanity can dominate their outlook reducing others to mere pawns in their game of power. We can all admit to knowing a few such souls!

Phlegmatic Temperament

The phlegmatic types lack the sparkle of the sanguine, but are most faithful. Unlikely to 'rock the boat' as the choleric and melancholic, they can be extraordinary scholars for neither passion nor the need for attention will cloud their judgement and speculation.

The phlegmatics have a degree of detachment that makes for great minds but does not foster warm relationships. They will be unlikely to offend others and equally unlikely to fall into the trap of judging others, but will often depart from a conflict situation with a sense of indifference. Where the sanguine's role is largely pastoral with active involvement, the phlegmatic is the solitary writer and scientist.

Such characters are slow but faithful workers. Since they are not annoyed easily or irritated by dire events they can be relied upon when times are difficult. A phlegmatic person often bears much common sense and mental profundity. Hence they are suited to scientific work and delicate research. If called upon they can be very heroic and sacrificial. Some eastern Europeans are well placed in this category.

On account of their slowness to react, however, they often let good opportunities slip away. They can be self-absorbed and thus selfish and not suited to community life. One of their more obvious flaws is laziness. In that case they need to be encouraged and motivated by others.

Those of phlegmatic temperament are likely to be stabilizing forces in any group situation. They will have a sense of duty and responsibility that will be a strong influence on their actions and decisions. In a group setting they, too, need positive influences from the authority figures or leaders. Where the sanguine is a conformist for the sake of acceptance, the equally obedient phlegmatic will be so from a sense of obligation and respect for tradition and the status quo. This can be a problem if the custom is false because they will not question those in authority.

Add virtue to your temperament

From what has been said, it should be evident that it is no easy task to form a perfect character. It is for us the work of a lifetime, for although the majority of persons are set in their characters before they reach the age of thirty, it is most rare that any character does not undergo modification and alteration during the entire lifetime of the individual.

In the formation of character we insist on proper education, good will, and the constant cultivation of those virtues that pertain to the state of life of the individual person. It is precisely here that the proper classification of our temperament is of great assistance. There is no point in trying to cultivate a specific virtue if it is diametrically contrary to our nature — that is, our temperament. It is pointless encouraging fortitude and frankness in a person well-endowed with a choleric temperament. They need to practise patience and meekness. It is the phlegmatic who needs courage and frankness.

Everyone is called to holiness. But the path that each must tread will vary, according to our vocation, our present moral status, and our temperament. All must climb the summit of perfection by different ways. The meek must become strong and the strong must become meek.

Each person is also called to chastity. The virtue of chastity, as we know, is a sub-virtue under the moral virtue of temperance. It varies in degrees and manner. The question thus arises to what degree are we called to be chaste? How do I practise this virtue of chastity? Before we answer these questions we need to know our temperament.

Here are a few steps to follow:

1. Concerning the temperaments, remember no one is a pure type; we are all a mixed blend but one type predominates.

2. We can sometimes guess our temperament but it is even better to ask someone who knows us really well, perhaps our parents or siblings, to classify our temperament, using some of the points above.

3. Once classified, list your strong points and weak points; e.g. if you are a sanguine-melancholic type then chastity may be more of a struggle for you.

4. Each person also has a predominant fault. Part of the package deal of original sin is our inherent predisposition to sin. We are morally weak in a particular vice that is often allied to our temperament, e.g. for the choleric it is pride. Here are the seven vices: pride, anger, envy, lust, greed, gluttony and sloth. What is yours?

The formation of character and the development to spiritual maturity as a person will depend ultimately on the cultivation and perfection of the virtues. Temperament is based more on physiological factors while character is psychological and ethical. Consequently, temperament is immutable, but it is the material out of which character is made, much in the same way as the marble or wood will be the material out of which a particular statue is fashioned. It is character that gives the formal distinction to the personality.

Consequently, the formation of character is closely associated with the psychology of habit formation and the theology of the virtues and vices. We have the power within ourselves to become sinners or saints, but whatever our choice, we will have to exert personal effort to achieve our goal. According to the ancient philosophers, a life of virtue was a guarantee of a life of happiness and perfection. The same is true in reference to the ideal character: it needs the balance and integration that are provided by the moral and intellectual virtues. For the perfect Christian, however, there is further required the gifts of the Holy Spirit. More about that later!

CHAPTER SIX
FULLY ARMED

In spite of the complexity of our human nature, we are now more aware of the various factors of our personality. We can appreciate where our faults and failings may lie, the source of our talents and the need for virtues. Being therefore prepared for combat, let us enter into battle: "Put on the armour of God that you may be able to stand against the wiles of the devil ... take the helmet of salvation, and the sword of the Spirit, which is the word of God" (Ephesians 5:11, 17).

The success of our spiritual battle requires knowledge of our enemy. I am not referring yet to the strategic methods of the Evil One, but the constant assault on our human nature from urges, impulses and temptations.

Puberty blues

When we were little, and I mean toddlers, to save water and time, we often washed or played together in the bath. Little children are at ease with their bodies and functions. Though they need to be taught modesty from the beginning, they accept these admonitions without much murmur.

As boys and girls grow, although they become more aware of their physical differences, there is little interest in the sexual domain. Instead the wonders of creation fascinate them. The world of imagination is all-pervasive; the building of sand-castles and being soldiers in the bush; the dressing up as nurses caring for the sick or being mothers at a tea party fill their busy days. This is childhood and these are the days of innocence.

At this stage of development, their spiritual formation should focus on basic virtues, such as honesty, modesty, generosity and kindness, good habits of prayer and a frequent and worthy reception of the Sacraments. Any sexual information at this premature stage can shatter their emotional development and disturb their natural serenity. On account of their cognitive and psychological immaturity, children cannot integrate the data and imagery of human sexuality in a moral and responsible manner. Besides they are just not interested! Parents are the best and only educators of their children in this domain and thus they know when it is most opportune to impart any knowledge. Thus, explicit sex education in primary school is a perversion of their innocence and maybe even an abomination before God.

The initial phase of adolescence, the teenage years, is marked by the transitional stage of puberty. In the sixth chapter of our document the *Truth and Meaning of Human Sexuality*, there is a whole section dedicated to puberty.

It is a time of self-discovery, of physical and psychological change. The biological changes warrant at the appropriate times, father and son, mother and daughter talks about the purpose of procreation, Marriage and family life. Teens growing up on farms receive nature's version that often simplifies matters. Accompanied with this information is the warm affirmation and acceptance of the physiological changes occurring in their own bodies. Without anxiety or fear, parents should explain any questions put before them on a need-to-know basis while restricting any compulsive urge to get it over and done with in one arduous session.

When appropriate, the basic purpose of genital organs needs to be explained by the parents lest there be any disinformation gained elsewhere. At this stage boys talk among themselves and the internet is a constant temptation. With appropriate material, the physiological development of the girl's cycle and male puberty should be presented in a serene manner and within the framework of Marriage by the respective parents.

It is within the context of the beauty of motherhood and the profound meaning of virginity that chastity and modesty will bear fruit in contrast to the hedonistic materialism portrayed in society. In like manner, fathers should challenge teenage boys, who can be vulnerable to erotic fantasies and sexual experiences, to recognize that their moral strength lies not in selfishness but in self-giving.

Positive information, hints on hygiene and an adequate teaching on the moral demands of God's law are some points that will require constant repetition. Youth need to be reminded of the sixth commandment and its moral demands. Place before them the story of the young man who sought out eternal life and was told by Jesus: "If you would enter life, keep the commandments" (Matthew 19:17). After listing them, Jesus challenged him in this positive manner: "You shall love your neighbour as yourself" (19:19). Adolescents are filled with tremendous energy that should be expended on others by practising the works of mercy, and in doing so they are freed from selfishness. Selfish desires at this stage of their lives quickly leads to lustful desires.

Frequent reception of the Sacraments and prayer fortify the soul against sin. Constant recourse to the Sacrament of Penance in particular will provide invaluable assistance in the formation of conscience and encouragement against the sins of the flesh. At this stage of development, masturbation can be a constant struggle, especially for the sanguine temperament who is perhaps more indulgent.

Impure impulses

During adolescence, with the development of sexual organs, there emerges desires and urges that need to be integrated. Indeed, we are all prone to sexual impulses at some time or another, irrespective of our age. The question that now needs to be addressed concerns the cause and morality of such impulses.

Around fifty years ago, the then Archbishop of Krakow,

in Poland, Karol Wojtyla, wrote a unique book, entitled *Love and Responsibility* (reprinted in 1993). Many today are aware of John Paul's teaching on sexuality under the title of *Theology of the Body*. The content of these discourses have been rediscovered and promoted by Christopher West, and more recently, Fr. Anthony Percy, in his *Theology of the Body Made Simple*. But perhaps many are unaware of its philosophical prototype. Wojtyla's profound text is truly a masterpiece in anthropology, sexual ethics and sexology.

At the beginning of *Love and Responsibility* the sexual instinct is discussed. Bishop Wojtyla prefers to refer to it as an 'urge' or 'impulse', because an 'instinct' is a reflex action common to animals—which we are not. Man is capable of rising above instinct in his actions unlike the beasts—though some of us can be very beastly at times. Then he adds a novel distinction that provides much consolation to adolescents. He says that the sexual urge is about what 'happens' in us at an involuntary level. At times there may be sexual arousal and interest that is not caused by our deliberate thoughts but just occurs or happens within us. This should not cause alarm, because there exists in us a natural disposition to desire, at a physical and psychological level, the opposite sex—provided that there is no core gender impairment. We possess an innate desire towards the opposite sex, towards another person who is to be loved. The sexual urge is the beginning of that attraction.

But the urge, on account of original sin, is prone to exploit pleasure for its own sake. In that regard the will needs to orient the desires, or better put, integrate these desires according to one's vocation and state in life. In doing so the sensual desires become subject to the love of the person and are not at the expense of the person, who can become an object of pleasure.

In order to be more specific, Wojtyla then unpacks the different forms of love to help us appreciate the higher domain of love to which we are all called in the communion of persons.

i. Love as attraction. This is the physical, emotional attraction between sexes. When spontaneous feelings arise for another they need to be integrated according to one's vocation. We are reminded that physical beauty is meant to lead us to the beauty of the person.

ii. Love as desire. This form of love as a desire is not a sensual longing for pleasure alone but for the person. A man is in need of a woman, for they fulfil each other and the sexual urge is oriented to this very purpose.

iii. Love as goodwill. When one loves the other for their own sake. It is a love that is not just good for me — but I want what is good for them. A genuine benevolent love is one that gives and surrenders itself to another without losing possession of the self. In giving of ourselves, we discover ourselves. This is the betrothal love of Marriage.

After making those subtle points, he then returns to the matter of the urge and what happens in man. We are reminded that our five external senses receive sense data or impressions. This data which is constantly being gathered elicits emotional responses. Advertising is based on this very presupposition — it is the key that unlocks the door of the heart and the wallet. The *smell* of French fries and the *sight* of McDonald's evoke emotional pleas from children who desire what their senses have already absorbed.

Sensuality and sex

We also can absorb the sense data of others as sexual beings. Women are very intuitive of others; almost like a radar they can zero in on another's emotional needs. Emotions react to values, however, and senses to content. At a fashion show, the models are dressed in such a manner so that what the eyes see elicits a particular response. Often that response, or sensate reaction, is emotional and sometimes physiological. If the response is sensual, orchestrated by the designers, then the person is valued as an 'object of desire'. That value is what we term sensuality. It refers to persons not as subjects but as potential objects of enjoyment. Because sensuality views another as an object of enjoyment instead of a person worthy of love, it can lead to the debasement of the dignity of the person.

The human person should never become an object to be used. Because the body is an integral part of the person, it must be viewed and treated with the respect that is owing to the person and not as if it were a detached appendage. Sensuality can devalue the person. Although sensuality is not an evil in itself, it poses a threat and a temptation.

Never forget that this sensual tendency, more prominent in men, is a direct result of original sin. In the beginning, before the Fall, our first parents were naked, unashamed and innocent. At that time, being in the state of grace, they were not tempted in the least to exploit each other's bodies. The difficulty of our post-Christian era is that advertising, films, the media market, wilfully exploit this inherent weakness in man for financial and other gains. How often does an advertisement on television or the internet portray the body of a woman in a sensual and immodest manner so as to coerce the viewer to buy this or that product?

Our fallen nature, although it may be weak and prone to sin, is not perverse or corrupt. When sense data is perceived, especially by the eyes in boys and the imagination in girls, and we feel the tug of sensuality to enjoy this sensation as an object of sexual pleasure, we need to do two things. Firstly, realize that this is a response of a fallen body to *raw material* or data. In itself, it is not sinful, but it has potential to sin. Sensual responses are fickle, they just happen in us, sometimes even inadvertently. Secondly, in order not to become sinful, we need to integrate the *raw material*. What does that mean? The word 'integrate' is derived from the Latin word *integrare* meaning to make whole or to put together. Thus, to integrate the sense data, we employ our will power, to assimilate those elements that will assist us in our vocation to love and discard that which induces us to lust.

In a certain manner, we give the raw material of our senses a moral form. Clay is formed by the potter into a given shape, raw vegetables are diced and formed by the chef into a set dish. We also need to integrate the sensual material according to our vocation and state of life so that we love the person as a person and not as an object of enjoyment.

Take, for example, a teenage boy who while walking past the pool sees a young girl immodestly dressed. Suddenly a sensual image has entered as raw material into his head and of its very nature provokes immediate pleasure. That image now needs to be integrated or it may lead him to sin. If the latter, he may turn and 'look' in an immoral manner at the girl and engage in impure thoughts and desires about her. Or he can say to himself, I need to keep walking and look straight ahead and distract my attention with some other thoughts. Conversely, he may think of his own sister who would not dress like that and may wonder if the poor girl has a brother or anyone who cares at home. As a result he may even say a prayer for her.

Girls also are prone to temptation but often it bears a different slant. A romantic DVD with immoral scenes or a saucy novel incites the imagination causing sexual arousal. Remember a faithful heart does not flirt with fantasies. Self-control means discipline of the inner thoughts and the imagination so that temptations are kept at bay. Saint Teresa of Avila called the imaginative power the 'crazy one'. Apart from making you crazy it can stimulate feelings and desires contrary to one's convictions. Once the mind is loosed from its moorings the heart is set adrift amid the waves of desire. Remember the saying: 'Empty hands are the work shop of the devil'. It means that when one is not busy at work or thinking in a constructive manner, the memory and imagination open themselves to temptations and fantasies about this romantic boy or ideal partner which can lead to emotional havoc and impure feelings.

Both scenarios require grace that bolsters the will power so that one achieves the successful integration of drives, feelings and thoughts. In turn, this results in the integration of one's sexuality (CCC 2345). When it becomes habitual then one can claim chastity as a virtue of his or her own.

Meaning of shame

After original sin, a sense of shame, an inward need to conceal ourselves from others, became a necessary component of our human nature. Our first parents were naked and unashamed in the beginning (Genesis 2:25). We, however, sense tremendous shame if our bodies are exposed to the public. There is an innate sense of privacy and reserve concerning our bodies that if violated tends to wound the inner fibre of our being. During the Second World War, the Gestapo would strip prisoners naked before others upon their arrival at a work camp, not only to claim their personal belongings, but also to extol their superiority by physical shame.

Clothes are natural to us because nakedness is unnatural. Shame is a natural protection for the body as an umbrella is a form of protection from the rain. Sexual shame is the concealment of sexual organs. It protects one from being exploited and used as an object of pleasure. It is for that reason that toddlers and children have no natural inhibitions about being naked because they have not yet attained puberty. Once that stage of maturation is reached, one becomes aware of sexual values.

In his masterpiece, *Love and Responsibility*, Karol Wojytla claims that modesty varies between the sexes. Girls seem to need more training in the ways of modesty—while men, he claims, possess a greater natural sense of modesty and shame because they are more sensual. At first glance, this supposition seems somewhat biased. What is being asserted, nevertheless, is a basic fact of life—so basic that it is often overlooked, especially in our immodest age. Man, being more sensual, places importance on the bodily parts of a woman and thus feels a greater sense of shame and, as a consequence, is more sensitive to the loss of modesty. On the other hand, girls who are less sensual may not be aware of their lack of modesty and thus need to be instructed regarding an appropriate dress code.

A lack of shame occurs when one acts towards another person in a way that the values of sex as such are given so much prominence that they obscure the essential value of the person, reducing him or her to an object of use or enjoyment. It is shamelessness that results in pornography that perverts the hearts of men and causes them to become predators instead of protectors of women.

Sentimentality and sex

Another domain of sexuality that warrants discussion is sentimentality. Most have heard of "The Sentimental Bloke," which reminds us of the classic Aussie, but that has nothing to do with this theme. Sentimentality in this context is akin to emotional romanticism. While sensuality is the value attributed to sense data, sentimentality is an emotional reaction to the sexual value residing in the whole person of the other sex. Men are sensually attracted to the bodily parts or shape of a woman. Women, however, are emotionally attracted to the whole of the man.

The manner of attraction is intense for the young who are seeking ideals and thus are in hot pursuit of romantic bliss. Some women suffer from sentimentality when the value attributed to the beloved is exaggerated out of all proportion — via the imagination and memory. It is for this reason that the Mills and Boon Series of fictional romance is so popular among the feminine gender. Apart from being mild entertainment or pulp fiction, as they say, it plays subtle havoc with the fantasy, our imaginative powers. As a result, the ideal of the person replaces the real which can later lead to disillusionment, marital trauma and divorce.

Instead of a sensual desire, sentimental love strives in a subjective manner for nearness, exclusivity and intimacy. The nearness, or closeness of heart, is primarily emotional and can endure extended period of physical separation, that, in turn, may romanticize further the ideal qualities of the other. Exclusivity implies that the beloved is sought for their own personal sake which may result in jealousy when in company. Sentimentality seeks intimacy in romantic love that provides tenderness and affirmation prior to any form of sexual expression.

The novelty of romantic love is very intense among the young and those of a sanguine temperament. One needs therefore to integrate one's feelings according to the objective reality of the individual and the actual situation.

Struggle against sin

Now that we appreciate the good qualities and the defects of the various temperaments and have understood that the formation of character is largely a personal choice, we are ready to tackle the issue of sin. Regardless of our background, learning and temperament, we are all weak and prone to sin and it is only by personal effort and God's grace that we are able to grow in grace and the virtues, in particular, chastity. Let's be honest, there exists in everyone's heart a tension between what they ought to be, and what they are. A real struggle exists between love of self and love of God.

What is sin? In the words of Saint Augustine: it is any thought, word, or deed against the law of God (CCC 1849). If we sin against our neighbour or even ourselves, that sin is primarily an offence against God. Also, let us not forget the dual causality of sin—by commission or omission: sins we have committed, or done, and sins that occur because we have failed to do that which we ought. Apart from actions, sins can also be of thoughts, desires and words.

Two of the Ten Commandments concern sins of desire—the ninth and tenth. These are the hidden sins (CCC 2534). Not to forget, of course, the eighth, which is about words ('bearing false witness'). By the way, regarding sins of the mouth, pick up your Bible and read what the Letter of Saint

James says about the mouth — "the tongue is fire" (James 3:6).

Sin is always a rejection, a failure, or a distortion of love that is charity. While we distinguish between objective and subjective sin, actual sin is always a personal sin. To commit a personal sin, three elements are required (CCC 1750):

1. Object of the action is morally wrong
2. Some knowledge that it is wrong
3. Deliberate consent.

According to the Bible and the Church's teaching, there are two degrees of sin: mortal sin (serious) and venial sin (light). We should use these two words to describe the two degrees of sin because this is the language employed by Scripture and the Church in the Catholic Catechism. In Saint John's first letter, he refers to the two types of sin and warns against sin that is mortal: "There is sin which is mortal (…) All wrongdoing is sin, but there is sin which is not mortal (1 John 5:16-17).

Effects of sin

What are the effects of these two types of sin? Firstly, mortal sin destroys God's love and sanctifying grace dies in the soul. God, on the other hand, still loves and wills the sinner's conversion. But that is why the Bible (1 John 5:16) and the Church uses the word mortal, *mors* being the Latin word for death.

Here is a detailed list of the tragic effects of mortal sin:

1. the loss of charity
2. privation of sanctifying grace
3. exclusion from Christ's kingdom
4. eternal death of hell [if there is no repentance] (CCC 1861).

If you think that the last point is over-the-top and perhaps a mistake, check out the section on hell in the Catechism and you will discover the startling fact that souls that go to hell are sinners who die in *unrepentant* mortal sin (CCC 1033). I chose 'hell' rather than being banished to hell because God does not send souls to hell as such, they go there because that is where they belong. When they die in mortal sin, devoid of grace, they possess no similarity to God, they have nothing in common with God, and therefore are unable to be with God in Heaven. As opposite ends of two magnets oppose each other, likewise when a godless soul encounters God it is repulsed to its own place (cf. Acts 1:25).

This is the teaching of Jesus Himself. When the rich young man asked about how to get to Heaven, the Lord told him not to sin, don't break the commandments: "You shall not kill. You shall not commit adultery…" (Matthew 19:18). Today people kill their babies, fornicate, commit adultery, take drugs and so on. In each case what is being done is a serious offence against God and thus a mortal sin, so unless such souls repent before death, their salvation is in the balance. Apart from sins committed there also are sins of omission, or neglect, which can be mortal: choosing not to attend Mass on Sundays; failing to provide due health care to a dying person; refusing to frequent Confession at least once a year when in mortal sin; failing to raise the children in the Catholic faith. Even sins of anger, gluttony, lying can be mortal. Any infringement of a commandment in a serious matter with knowledge and full consent is a mortal sin.

The main difference between mortal and venial sin is that what is being done is less serious, or it may be serious but done without full knowledge or complete consent. Here are the effects of venial sin:

1. it weakens charity
2. it manifests disordered affection for things
3. it impedes progress in the exercise of the virtues
4. it predisposes us to mortal sin
5. it merits temporal punishment (CCC 1863).

Venial sin weakens God's grace in our souls but it does not destroy that grace nor love of God in our souls. Daily we struggle against venial sins; our selfishness, pride and laziness are indication of self-love before love of God and neighbour.

The Church is full of sinners who think they are saints, and saints who think they are sinners. Overall, sinners are actually more numerous. Sinners, like ourselves—for we are all sinners—can be classed according to four groups: the neglectful, the weak, the wilful, and the malicious.

a. Sinners who are blissfully ignorant or indifferent, that should do better but don't. They are careless, and often it is suffering or death that brings them to their knees.

b. Then there are the weak sinners; those who give in to their sensual desires, such as the sanguine type, and lack the will power to do otherwise. Being more weak than wicked, they respond well to a strong sermon and rally when encouraged.

c. The third class of sinners are those who justify their sinful ways and seek allies in their wickedness. Their conversion is difficult, because their hearts are hardened and so devoid of God's grace that they seek not even the mercy of God.

d. The last class of sinners are those of true malice and diabolical pride. Both heart and soul have fallen into the abyss of apostasy by defecting from the faith which induces them to perverse morality. These individuals are beyond the arguments of reason or human endeavours but only fasting, prayer and supernatural intervention can achieve their salvation.

Imperfections and the perfect

Before we close this heavy-duty chapter, it would profit us to mention moral imperfections. Our physical constitution readily admits many imperfections which explain the need for hairdressers, beauty salons, cosmetics, gyms and whatever else pampers our vanity and reduces our waistline. Apart from these bodily blemishes, there also exist moral imperfections that need to be distinguished from venial sins. While sin is intrinsically evil in itself, no matter how insignificant some may regard it, imperfections are faults and flaws in our character.

Wherein lies the difference between sin and imperfection? Sin of its nature is always an offence against God in thought, word or deed, when we break one of the commandments. To commit a sin, however, we also need two other elements, one is knowledge and the other is wilfulness. When we know what we are doing is wrong and we still choose to do it, we sin. Anything less is an imperfection. So all those unwilled aberrations of the mind and thoughts that just happened early in the morning when someone else made you wait for your breakfast were imperfections.

Many imperfections are the result of a lack of charity or a weakness in our temperament. The melancholic tends to sadness while the sanguine quickly angers. Sometimes imperfections bind the soul because of a particular attachment, which may in itself not be sinful, but can lead to sin. A daily attachment to alcohol could lead to dependency and one who insists on having the last word in every conversation may become proud and arrogant. Some people are prone to laziness and thoughtless of the needs of others, while some are always being critical as self-appointed prophets of doom and gloom.

Over time, even the best portrait often gets cracks in the paint, a worn canvass and a bland dullness in colour. A skilled artist can remedy many a flawed painting to return it to its pristine condition. So, too, we need to let the Divine Artist shape our character and reduce the rough edges of our personality so that we advance spiritually.

Whatever our imperfections, prayer, humility and a sound examination of conscience can bring to the surface those areas in need of spiritual maintenance. If we do not rid ourselves of habitual imperfections, we shall not attain perfection in this life. Remember, we are saints in the making and it is for this reason that our goal is complete transformation in Christ so that we can boast with Saint Paul: "It is no longer I who live, but Christ who lives in me" (Galatians 2:20).

CHAPTER SEVEN
TEMPTATION AND SIN

We seek spiritual chastity so that we can enter into the communion of persons with self-giving love. We also know that this quest requires the integration of our sexuality by means of our will power. Such an endeavour involves an awareness of our fallen state and an inner knowledge of our moral character and temperamental dispositions.

Since chastity is the key that opens the heart to true love it takes particular prominence in our study. We can classify chastity as a spiritual energy capable of defending love from the perils of selfishness. It is a spirit-filled power for it is accompanied with divine grace. In our attempt to attain self-mastery we not only need God's power but also we must be mindful of the presence of our spiritual foes. *"He that is aware of the snares shall be secure"* (Proverbs 11:15).

When the Lord Jesus formulated the Lord's Prayer, He provided in the seventh petition, the last one, a stark reminder of the power of Satan: 'Deliver us from evil [the Evil One].' In our battle, we should be aware of the tactics of Satan and the manner in which he seeks to devour souls. Disintegrated sexuality and unchaste living is his forté and many souls perish on account of sins of the flesh.

Before we explain his tactics, let us set aside a few common references to diabolical activity. Firstly, when someone says to you that 'the spirit made me do it,' you should ask yourself: 'Which one?' There are three spirits: *the divine Spirit, the diabolical spirit,* and *the human spirit.* God always inclines us to the good; the devil always inclines us to evil, though often via a seemingly 'good' work; and the human spirit may be inclined to evil or to good, depending on motives, habits and desires.

Diabolical Spirit

Some people don't believe in Satan or the Devil. But then again, some people do believe in Santa Claus and Easter Bunnies. What we should believe is that which the Church and the Bible teach. Both are emphatic that Satan and his demons exist as fallen angels and that they seek to conquer God's Kingdom. Since we are his temples, humans are prime targets of him whom Christ called, "a murderer from the beginning ... a liar and the father of lies" (John 8:44).

We need to avoid two extremes concerning the devil. One position denies his existence outright. The other blames the devil for everything that goes wrong. When caught drunk-driving, some blame the devil instead of self. Others may claim that demons cause them to drink or that their drug addiction is the result of a trans-generational curse. This is false. In short, the devil cannot *control* us, because we have free will. So as a rule, diabolical influence over an individual Christian is largely restricted to temptations. The major part, therefore, of this chapter will discuss how we are tempted. Also diabolic obsession and possession need to be mentioned here.

Diabolic obsession is rare. It occurs when the devil externally torments a person in an intense and repeated manner. More than likely, the tormented soul is a holy and virtuous person. It can take various forms. Saint John Vianney, the Parish Priest of Ars in France, suffered much at night from frightening noises in the house, howling dogs and frightful attacks. An Italian Franciscan mystic, Saint Padre Pio, recently canonized in 2001, was often physically bashed and bruised at night by demons when he was a young man.

Obsession need not be physical; it can affect the

imagination and the five external senses. Yet one must be careful not to attribute to a diabolical cause what is human or drug-induced. Attacks, external or internal in the mind, can result in anger, despair and sensuality. So we need to battle against such assaults with prayer, trust in God and sacramentals such as holy water and medals. Numerous saints have been tempted by deceptive visions, as, for example, Saint Teresa who would see an 'angel of light' or at other times, horrific and perverse forms.

Diabolical infestation is when a place or area manifests demonic activity. In that case, a priest may bless a house or locality, invoking God's protection while sprinkling holy water. Even when we have no special problems, but to *prevent* the influence of the devil, it is a good practice to have our house blessed, say, once a year.

Diabolical possession, on the other hand, is even rarer than obsession. It occurs when God permits the devil to invade the body of a person. When Satan occupies a body, he cannot dominate the spiritual powers of the will and intellect but he can use the bodily faculties and powers. His control is spasmodic and often violent. Evil persons, such as Rasputin, the Russian pseudo-monk during the reign of the Czars, possessed exceptional bodily strength and power that defied natural ability. Recently, the film *The Exorcism of Emily Rose,* based on the true story of Annalise Michel, faithfully portrayed the state of a possessed soul. Only when a possessed case is declared, after rigorous investigation, does the Church employ the Rite of Exorcism. Clearly the Sacraments of Penance and Holy Communion are powerful antidotes, in addition to fasting and prayer (Matthew 17:20).

At the same time, we must be careful not to attribute to the devil what is an unusual phenomenon but may have natural causes. Some of these may be the result of physiological or constitutional ailments, an overly active imagination, drug abuse, depression, and especially mental illnesses and nervous disorders. While the melancholic temperament is most prone to illusion in mystical matters because of introversion, the sanguine type also can be easily misled regarding mystical phenomena in the affective domain.

Before we close this section, let's list some theological facts concerning the diabolical:

1. demons are spirit creatures who are fallen angels.

2. demons can only invade and torment us by God's permissive will.

3. demons cannot control the human will.

4. angels and demons can act upon the imagination and other internal and external senses and what is material.

5. demons cannot cause true miracles but only do tricks and feats, create visions, falsify ecstasy, tears, healings and imitate divine power.

6. demons concentrate much of their energy on temptation.

Satan—in Search of Prey

We are all weak humans, easily misled and confused. If Satan is likened to a hunter who is in search of prey, then he pursues us with stealth, noting our weaknesses and calculating our moves. He is the master of seduction who patiently plots our fall. In the Synoptic Gospels (Matthew, Mark, Luke), we read about the temptations of Christ. We note how Satan waited until Our Lord was hungry before he tempted Him with food. Like an expert hunter, be assured—especially if you are pursuing a chaste life—that Satan, like an expert hunter who is shrewd and brilliant, is watching and waiting for you. He prepares his assault from afar, ready to strike you when you least expect it or when your guard is down.

First, he wants to disarm you from prayer, which is your armour and protection. Once you are more vulnerable, he gradually chips away at the fortress of your soul. Slowly but surely, he encourages imperfections by suggesting that you are too harsh on yourself. There is no need to go to Confession, and after all, others don't go and they are *good* people. In time, those imperfections become venial sins that further distance you from grace and sanctity.

In order to tempt you into mortal sin, he masquerades evil as good. He sets the bait with exceptional care and provides the exact place, occasion, and circumstances. Seduction requires a snare that we can call an occasion of sin. How many young people every weekend frequent pubs and discos. Some of them may think that there is no evil in such places. It is true that the building, as such, is not evil. Yet, it is also true that in those places, late at night, drugs, alcohol, deafening music, empty conversations, obscene language, immodest clothing and sensual body dancing are instrumental tools of the Evil One that degrade our sexuality.

Add to this seduction his carefully chosen clientele, who are shrewdly placed before you as counsellors and friends. God has his servants, and Satan has his slaves. Some are patently aware of it; many, however, are not, for they are slaves primarily of sin and useful tools of his trade. One inmate of a security prison which I used to visit, remarked how corrupt young men became after being in jail with hardened criminals. These young ones left prison, after serving a term for drink driving, with an adept knowledge of and inclination for criminal activity, not to mention additional contacts.

Cast a backward glance over your life and recall how many times you were initiated into evil by the advice, behaviour and conduct of your mentors or companions. On many occasions it was the encouragement of 'friends' that enticed you to drink or to indulge in sexual exploits. Some of them may appear as good people, as Christians, to offer help when you were depressed or troubled. In the Old Testament, Job when troubled was tempted to sin by three counsellors who came to offer him their assistance. In the end, he provided them with counsel (see Job 3-31).

Trials and temptations

Temptations are not sins in themselves. Yet they can incite or predispose us to sin. If you play with fire, eventually you'll be burnt. Toy with temptations and in the end you will succumb. On the other hand it is by overcoming temptations with virtue that we grow stronger and holier. It is by competing with better tennis players on the court that one's game improves.

Every temptation presents itself as an attractive offer to the mind. Before Satan can enter your heart as he did the heart of Judas (see John 13:27), he must knock on the door of your mind. All temptations begin with a thought in your mind or as an image that evokes pleasure. Once the mind has assented to the temptation, the will consents and at that very precise moment we sin and grace is lost.

In addition, when we frequent 'occasions of sin' we are weakened. An occasion of sin is that place, time, thing or person that predisposes us to sin. Such situations weaken the effect of sanctifying grace in our souls and lessen the defence of virtue in our wills and minds. Take, for example, a young man who is addicted to internet pornography. At this moment in his life he has a specific moral weakness that needs assistance, grace and the virtue of chastity. It would thus be an occasion of sin for *him* to surf the net *alone* in his bedroom.

Some years ago, a priest visited an ex-alcoholic who was once the town drunk. He had given up the drink over twenty-two years ago. Being a most affable and easy-going type, the priest was surprised one Monday evening to find him rather distressed at home. After some time, the clergyman kindly said: "What is bothering you tonight?" He replied in a tense tone: "On the weekend my nephew was visiting and stayed the night, which was fine, but on Sunday he forgot to take his grog with him. There is half a cask of wine in the fridge – and the temptation is driving me so insane I can't even open the fridge door." He added: "I am an alcoholic – each day and only for the day I promise myself not to touch the stuff. To be alone here with that alcohol there is too great a temptation." The priest said: "Would you like me to get rid of it?" With much relief, he answered: "Please, take it away from here." The wine was a near occasion of sin for this man, too near to bear. Although he remained strong, he also knew his limits.

Doubtful dating

Many young people's first sexual experience occurs during their first few dates. Did you know that dating is a recent novelty? Yes, in the past people avoided these temptations – they courted instead. Some claim too that serial dating results in serial divorcing. This might sound extreme unless your definition of 'dating' involves casual sex and cohabitation.

Against this backdrop of tragic temptations beams a ray of hope - a romantic novel. The author, Carmen Marcoux, is a Catholic mother of seven, who found time - I know not how - to write a book on chastity. As it turned out, the novel, *Arms of Love*, is a classic Catholic romance that has won the hearts of millions since its publication in 2002.

Basically the plot is a story of Christian courtship. Yes, even non Catholic Christians would love the plot but find it challenging. Joanie, a strong Catholic woman, setting out in a new career as a journalist, must face one of the greatest challenges of her young life . . . romance. Joanie finds herself attracted to the handsome young commercial producer, Brandon, but he is a 'neo pagan' in need of finding God. And Joanie won't compromise her love of Jesus. So Brandon must shape up or ship out!

The book faithfully presents the Church's teachings on Marriage and the Sacraments, not to mention Sacramentals. Besides the romance it also parades chastity in modern and refreshing manner. Joanie is chaste but not a prude. She is an ideal yet human model for chastity which is ultimately a selfless love of neighbour. The opposite of love is not hate, it is selfishness. Chastity is the way to put love into practice in our relationships both before marriage and after marriage. Even married couples are called to conjugal chastity (cf. CCC 2348-2450).

Courting versus dating

The novel highlights the pivotal distinction between dating and courtship. A person would never enter into a courtship with someone whom they would not consider marrying; yet a person will often enter a dating relationship with someone to whom they are attracted while knowing that they would never want to marry that person. The problem arises when emotional commitment and often physical intimacy lead a couple who are dating to consider marriage and even pursue it, only later to decide that it was the wrong decision.

Young unmarried people are mistaken when they think that the key question in intimacy is 'how far can we go?' The question itself indicates a flawed outlook. In short, reserve your affection and guard physical intimacy so that you are not igniting passions that are intended to be reserved for marriage. The novel is filled with intimate yet pure moments that will provide practical guidelines for young unmarried couples. The idea, of course, is to save yourself in all ways for marriage so that you can someday reap the manifold blessings of a truly holy and passionate marriage . . . the way it was designed to be, by God. It is a great insurance plan for fidelity.

Accountability is one of the more unique traits of the novel. It is human nature for us to strive harder to achieve a goal when we know someone will be checking up on our progress. If we have to answer to someone else, we tend to be more focussed. If not their parents a couple should seek out at least one mentoring couple whom they trust. There are many exciting new emotions that come into play when a couple enters a courting relationship, but there are also many challenges. A good mentoring couple will guide the younger couple, helping to keep them on track while sharing with them the joys and struggles that they face.

As much as possible, a courtship should take place in the heart of the home. The family plays a critical role in your relationship, and the support of family throughout the years is an indispensable gift for a marriage. Getting involved in family functions and doing things with parents and siblings will often increase respect for parents and the role of parenting. Involvement with family is also an ideal way to spend time together without the temptation to compromise your decision to reserve physical intimacy!

As a story for promoting chastity within a contemporary setting, those who enter into the witty and provocative life of Joanie and Brandon will be swept along on a splendid love story, and yet there remains another dimension worthy of note. Throughout the novel there is a powerful theme of forgiveness. In moral matters what often does matter is: How can I be forgiven; how can I start again. The book examines and resolves at diverse levels forgiveness in a most incisive manner.

Lastly, this book is not merely for teens but also for parents and grandparents who know and advise the younger generation. Since its publication a sequel has arrived called *Surrender*, which is about the first years of married life. It provides much guidance to help one live out purity in the world today.

Prey or prayer

Periodically, we can be assailed by the most perverse thoughts, a barrage of images that may plague our imagination without any provocation. We are under attack and we need strength to stand firm. Provided we do not will or consent to these images and desires, then we have not sinned. One may wonder, however, why such 'happenings' occur. Be consoled that the saints have trodden this thorny path. With each victory the soul is embellished with greater virtue. Also, take consolation in the fact that you must be a good person if Satan regards it as worth his while to torment you in this manner.

Satan is most seductive in how he ensnares the heart and deceives the mind. And although he is powerful, only God is all-powerful. We must remind ourselves time and time again that Satan can only tempt us, and with Christ we are able to do all things. Moreover, the Lord has prayed for us that we might not be overpowered (John 17:15).

Once Satan has disarmed us from prayer and Sunday Mass, he often employs the tactic of self-pity to seduce us. Let us now analyse his methodology concerning lust. Sins of the flesh, such as fornication and adultery, are too often committed and the seduction is commonplace.

First, one just does not commit a mortal sin of this calibre by accident. We just don't wake up one morning and decide to commit adultery, to render asunder the holy bonds of fidelity and loyalty. Be assured that before the deadly assault of lust, there were a series of lost skirmishes.

If one were to list them, they might appear in this order:

a. Dissatisfaction - married life has become a boring routine

b. Frictional relations - about money, children, personal issues

c. Recourse in the memory to past hurts and unresolved matters

d. Fantasies in the imagination begin about the ideal partner

e. Romantic desires of the heart emerge when tired or depressed

f. Encounters occur with an understanding and sympathetic friend

g. Infatuation - new feelings emerge regarding this 'ideal' companion

h. Lustful thoughts and desires are entertained about him or her

i. Adulterous acts happen with the 'ideal' companion *then, hopefully with grace...*

j. Sense of betrayal and infidelity initiates a conversion

k. Guilt and remorse induces one to seek forgiveness.

Some couples would admit that stages a - d occur periodically in their Marriage. Yet admittance or discernment of each step needs to be checked and integrated. All temptations must be combatted, fought with vigour and defeated. If they are not routed at the outset then they take root and induce us farther down the path of lust. If we are a sanguine type who enjoys romance novels with a carefree imagination, then we must take particular care, for we are easy prey to seduction.

Lust and marital infidelity is one of Satan's specialties. Let us take, for example, a married man who commits adultery while on a business conference. At the outset, this man is out of his routine, away from home and so he lets his guard down, not to mention his prayer life. No longer is he vigilant nor does he have his routine as a buffer to protect him. During the weekend away, Satan reminds him of a recent fight he had with his wife and tempts his memory to focus on past hurts. After a few drinks, late one night, he vividly recalls his wife's recent comments and he begins to feel sorry for himself. He wonders why he ever married her and perhaps if they would have been happier if they had never met. Self-pity is one of Satan's best devices.

Often we need an excuse to justify moral disorder and to unleash the desires of lust. Self-pity provides us with that excuse. At the table, one of his colleagues knowingly smiles at him. For years they have been friends and she appreciates his company. After having granted liberty to his license via self-pity, Satan now tempts him to think that he deserves better, that he has had it tough over the years and that God would not expect anything more of him. Once he consents to this deceptive logic, anything becomes plausible. He may even conclude that a little affair could be beneficial to his marriage. The rest is history!

Another sin of the sexual domain that causes profound angst is masturbation. It is called many things, onanism (cf. Genesis 38:6-10), an impure act or self-abuse. The last is true to type because it is an abuse of self, often caused by selfishness and a lack of true charity. When Our Lord condemned "*looking lustfully at a woman*" (Mt 5:28), He obviously intended any external actions which add to lust's intensity and expression.

In the Catechism the matter is well outlined (CCC 2352). Although it is often held to be more common among males, they being more sensual, both sexes are prone to commit this sin which is simply the deliberate stimulation of the genital organs in order to gain sexual pleasure. The word deliberate is most important. For if sexual pleasure came during one's sleep, or by accident, then it is not sinful. The Church and the Bible teach that masturbation is a mortal sin. It violates God's law that sexual pleasure belongs to the marital act of intercourse between husband and wife. The sexual act consists of two inseparable dimensions: the unitive: the union of male and female, and the procreative: being open to co-operate in the creation of new life. Masturbation fails to involve either one of those dimensions.

Some 'experts' do not regard masturbation as sinful, a grave moral disorder, claiming that it is a normal phenomenon of sexual development. This claim cannot be supported by ethics, psychology or theology. Our age is besotted with sex! It incites sexual immorality and refuses to acknowledge the value of chastity. An age of lust is one that is devoid of true love. Self-giving love is the only option for true happiness, not self-indulgence. When masturbation becomes habitual, one is often self-absorbed and narcissistic, which is an impediment to true love. Masturbation leads to lust, and lust is fuelled by pornography which exploits and debases the person. One's maturity and psychological stability, however, are factors that may lessen subjective responsibility in this action.

Guidelines to Stay on Track

Here are some solutions to assist with masturbation.

a) Foster a discipline of self-control by the law of freedom (James 1:25). Remind oneself that the soul controls the body, we are not slaves of the flesh. It is in giving that we receive joy. It is in exercising will power over our desires that we 'feel' truly liberated.

b) Practise mortification of pleasure drives by means of self-denial. All people mortify their desires at one stage or another. Sportsmen control their eating habits and sexual desires for the sake of the game. We are in the game of life and we need to deny ourselves certain pleasures so as to strengthen our will power and exercise dominion over our imagination.

c) Chastity requires grace and thus daily prayer is essential. If we don't pray, we shall not succeed. As a minimum, at least three Hail Marys before going to bed at night. Even better, start to pray the Rosary each day. Ask your Guardian Angel, who does exist, to protect you from all harm and temptations.

d) Avoidance of all occasions of sin, e.g., internet, films, magazines. Even a quick flick through magazines or brief surfing of some sites on the net will result in failure. Once the eyes have absorbed lustful images, sensual desires are stirred.

e) Frequent Confession is an absolute necessity. The Sacrament of Penance heals the soul of its lustful desires and provides those graces we need to overcome temptations. We should never be embarrassed to confess our impure acts or desires — even on a weekly basis. God knows all our sins, after all! The priest will never be disgusted by what you say, for he himself must practise chastity and will listen to far worse sins than yours. One helpful hint is that we must always confess the number of occurrences and the type of sexual sin. For example, don't say in Confession: "I was impure!" One must be specific, for example: 'I performed two impure acts by myself' or 'I had one impure desire and sexual intercourse twice with my girlfriend.' If you are not precise regarding the sin, the priest is obliged, like a surgeon who is cutting out a tumour, to dig deeper by means of questions to locate the exact nature of the sin so as to impart appropriate penance and absolution.

f) Frequent Holy Communion is essential for spiritual protection. Whenever possible, provided we are spiritually prepared (free of mortal sin and fasting for one hour beforehand), we should receive the Sacrament of the Eucharist. "If anyone eats of this bread, he will live for ever" (John 6:51). Also, the effort you make to provide spiritual nourishment for your soul by attending Holy Mass offsets the clamour of your body for physical pleasures.

g) Regular guidance from a Confessor or Spiritual Director. As the priest is well-trained in chastity and understands the daily struggle to be pure, he is an ideal resource for guidance and encouragement. Furthermore, when approached in Confession you have the assurance of anonymity and absolute confidentiality guaranteed by the Seal of Confession.

h) Self-abuse or masturbation is an inordinate love of self. So it needs to be offset by: (i) giving yourself to others so that you think less of your own needs or problems and more of the plight and suffering of those around you. Join a soup kitchen which feeds the homeless once a week or do some volunteer work at the St Vincent de Paul shop; and (ii) pursuing activities that enable you to express yourself in a positive and creative way such as hobbies, activities and interests that will occupy your time and benefit others.

i) Never give up and never presume it is under control. It may be a daily struggle with many falls throughout the week. Well, go to Confession more often, ask for more advice, pray more often, but never give up. When the car is bogged down to the axle, the winch once secured only gradually pulls out the vehicle. It takes time to break free from a vice, to conquer a bad habit. It may take months, it may take years, but never give up. Also, never think that you will never fall again. Be always on your guard: "the devil prowls around like a roaring lion, seeking someone to devour" (1 Peter 5:8).

Fornication deforms true love

Another common sin against chastity is fornication. When I was a teenager, it was called 'living in sin'; now it is simply called 'living together'. We seemed to have dropped the sin aspect somewhere.

Again the Catechism reminds us that this action, the sexual union between an unmarried man and an unmarried woman is a mortal sin (CCC 2363). Some may assert that this is because the Church is against sex, for priests are 'forced' to be celibate. Leaving aside the mythical misconceptions regarding celibacy that is freely chosen 'for the sake of the kingdom' (Matthew 19:10), the reasoning behind the sinfulness of pre-marital sex lies in Heaven. It is God's teaching, after all, and He wants us to protect our sexuality from misuse or abuse. He established this boundary line that forbids sexual relations outside of Marriage. If we cross the line then we turn away from God, forfeit His grace and if we do not repent we lose the game of life and Heaven: "neither fornicators, nor idolaters, nor adulterers shall possess the kingdom of God" (1 Corinthians 6:10).

Living together is a common practice today. Cohabitation, which is the same thing, does create emotional bonding and a sense of commitment to each other in the relationship, and yet it lacks the permanent and public commitment of Marriage. Often people say: 'Isn't it a good idea to live together before you marry to make sure that you are compatible? Surely it's best to test your love first, before taking the plunge!'

God has designed us in a particular way with a set of moral norms according to our human nature—called the Ten Commandments—of which one demands that sexual intercourse belong only to those who are married. Such a teaching is not anti-sexual but appreciates in a positive way that sexual intercourse is the fullest physical expression of love between a couple and of its very nature is able to create new life (CCC 1643, 2360-2363). The total and mutual gift of self in this manner is an expression of an already willed commitment we call Marriage.

Many claim that living together gives you a true idea of married life. Yet Government Statistics illustrate that the longer a couple cohabitate before Marriage, the greater the likelihood they will divorce later. Why? Because both true love, and death, have one thing in common: you cannot try them out beforehand. If you want to try out a parachute, the only real way to experience it is to jump out of a plane. Anything less doesn't work. All the training before that first jump is nothing compared to the real thing. The same is true with Marriage, you cannot just try it out; there are no 'high flights' that convey the real experience of living as husband and wife.

Living together before Marriage is a great risk. Why? Because such couples are sexually active and thus find it difficult to break up if they are not really suited. Once one is emotionally involved it becomes hard to separate, even when one knows deep down that he or she is not meant for me. On the other hand, if one has remained chaste, that is, practised self-control, then one is not so involved and it is easier to separate with less emotional trauma, if things are not meant to work out (see section on chastity in CCC 2337-2345).

'But sex is natural and I love this person,' some may say. Yes sexual desires are natural. But they are a part of a whole. Just as doors belong to a house, our sexual drives belong to our sexuality, our personhood, which are gifts from God. To isolate and use our sexual powers when we are not yet married is dishonest and harmful. It's making a part more important than the whole! Sex is not more important than true love.

Furthermore, just because a desire exists doesn't justify its satisfaction. Besides, just think of the damage the pill is doing to a woman's body. Or the children that are aborted in the name of free sex. Remember, true love is total love, not a fraction. Sex for mere physical pleasure is wrong because a person should never be used for pleasure — a person is not an object of enjoyment. True love doesn't take or grab but gives of itself in a permanent, exclusive and faithful way — which means Marriage.

In 2005, Anne-Marie Ambert of the Vanier Institute, in Ottawa, Canada completed a study on *"Cohabitation and Marriage: How are they related?"* Her results claim that cohabitation leads to a higher divorce rate. The longer a couple live together first, the greater the risk of divorce. The increased rate of divorce, Ambert asserts, is caused by insecurity, failure to make a commitment, few communication skills and lack of fidelity. The study illustrated that unfaithfulness was the most significant factor leading to divorce. Marriage is a real commitment for real lovers. It's more than just a piece of paper. Marriage is a permanent, faithful and exclusive bond (covenant) of love.

Personalist love

We are called to love according to the personalist norm. This first of all requires affirmation of the value of the person. Reverence for the dignity of the person precedes the attraction to the sexual values of another. Love is directed not towards 'the body' nor towards 'a human being of the other sex,' but precisely towards a person. What is more, only when it is directed to the person is love true love. Love is not an emotion or sensation. It is an act of the will.

This leads to the self-giving characteristic of betrothal love, a love based on reciprocity, friendship, and rooted in commitment to a common, shared good. Sexual relations are in accord with the personalist norm only when they occur between persons who are already completely united in Marriage. Before the love of man and woman can take on its definitive form, become 'betrothal love,' the man and the woman each face the choice of the person on whom to bestow the gift of self — their own will, body and emotions. The object of choice needs to be another person because they are a person.

Lastly, sexual encounters before marriage can awaken a lustful desire for variety, which may endanger a future Marriage. And if one hasn't been able to control one's sexual desires before Marriage, what about afterwards? Marriage requires self-control too, especially when the husband or the wife is sick or absent. When sex is not unveiled before Marriage it is precious, intimate and mysterious. Chastity before Marriage and faithfulness after, that's the formula for success.

Here is a summary of four reasons against fornication.

1. It is against God's commandments. Sexual intercourse belongs in marriage alone (see Ex 20:14; Deut 5:18; Mt 15:19; 19:18; Rom 13:9; Col 3:5; Eph 5:3). Sex outside of marriage, being sinful, is called fornication: "Do not err; neither fornicators, nor idolaters, nor adulterers shall possess the kingdom of God" (1 Corinthians 6:10).

2. Sexual actions are a part of the total gift of self which is marriage. Outside of marriage there is a lack of total self-giving. So pre-marital sex is a lie.

3. It can put pressure on a couple to marry when they may not be really suited.

4. It increases the probability of divorce because it prevents God's grace from entering into the relationship and leads to selfishness and infidelity.

Devilish discouragement

Falling into temptation and then consenting to mortal sin is a complete and utter catastrophe, but there always remains hope. Charity and God's abiding presence in the soul is lost, but not all is lost. Once we have sinned in this manner, God's mercy offers us the possibility of forgiveness. His voice, deep within our conscience, invites us to repent and make reparation. Although sins of malice denote a hardening of the heart, sins of the flesh, after the grace of contrition, allow for immediate revival. Sadly, His voice is not the only one seeking our attention.

Satan acts quickly to consolidate his victory; he fears the sorrow of the sinner. First, he tempts the sinner at any cost to postpone making a good confession. Then, he desires that we minimize the sin committed, or even excuse it altogether by suggesting several extenuating circumstances. After all, why would we confess to a priest who may also commit sins of the flesh. Such indiscretions, he whispers in our imagination, are all too common. Only prudes would class *that* as a serious sin.

Whatever subtle manoeuvres are employed by Satan, the ultimate weapon is discouragement. While the embers of conscience are burning there is always the possibility of penitential ignition. So the Seducer employs his ultimate weapon of assault, that is, discouragement. Our imagination begins to say: 'Why not give it all up and find some peace! You tried to be chaste, and you did your best, but nobody can do the impossible.' In order that we become slaves of sin, Satan wants us to be bound in chains; hence the word vice, a bond that is nearly impervious to the presence of divine grace. So he pushes us to the abyss and beckons us to surrender. 'What hope have you now? Why bother trying to go back, you are not able to start again, not after what you have done? You really don't believe that He will forgive you or that you are able to be forgiven?'

In Scripture, Satan is sometimes called 'the accuser' (Revelation 12:10). Before the very eyes of our mind he enlarges the sins we have committed, that he himself tempted us to commit. His aim is to make us doubt God's forgiveness, as if our past is beyond the realm of redemption. In spiritual combat, we must stand firm and trust in God.

If we have confessed our sins in the Sacrament of Penance, then they are forgiven if we have contrition. Although the accuser insinuates doubts concerning God's mercy, we need to believe not in feelings but in facts. It is a fact that Jesus forgives and forgets. Think about these words spoken to the woman caught in adultery: "Neither do I condemn you, go and sin no more" (John 8:11). Or the words of the dying thief, who stole Heaven on Good Friday: "Truly, I say to you, today you will be with me in Paradise" (Luke 23:43). Believe the facts of faith, not doubts or feelings (CCC 2005).

CHAPTER EIGHT
PURE PERFECTION

We are certain that purity is associated with holiness. It is impossible to find an impure saint. Are we not called to serve Our Lord in "holiness and justice" (Luke 1:75) and this holiness denotes the virtue of purity. Saint Thomas Aquinas claimed that sanctity implies purity because is it derived from the Greek word *agios* meaning unsoiled or, better put, uncontaminated. The pure are those who are devoid of stain, which is a code word for sin, and the citizens of Heaven are sinless as are all the saints. So somehow between now and then, between time and eternity, we need to become pure, for only the pure and perfect enter Heaven: "You, therefore, must be perfect, as your heavenly Father is perfect" (Matthew 5:48). "Nothing unclean shall enter into Heaven" (Revelation 21:27).

Every year this theme is repeated on the Solemnity of All Saints when the Church reminds us of purity and its inseparable link with holiness. After the readings that bear this hallmark, the Gospel on the Beatitudes is proclaimed (Matthew 5:1-11). When we listen to the words: 'Blessed are the pure for they shall see God,' we are reminded that purity has as its final goal, God, our ultimate end.

I have only met a handful of people who did not want to go to Heaven and be with God. Our hearts are geared for perfect happiness, and God delivers that package deal in Heaven. In the past, most knew and believed that basic fact, but today I am not so sure. One elderly man that I visited in a nursing home was most willing to talk to me about anything and everyone except God. Every time I even came close to mentioning religion, Church or eternity he became angry and insisted that I change the conversation. At our last encounter, as I was leaving, I said: 'Let me give you a blessing, it's free, costs you nothing and will help you!' — for he was in some physical pain. Yet he adamantly refused even a blessing. He died the very next day. There was no funeral, no prayers, only a cremation with instructions to cast his remains to the four winds. What a grim entrance into eternal life!

Purity and preservation

Many die as they have lived. We want to live for the Lord and die in His grace so that we shall dwell forever in His domain. Purity is a key component that will ensure a successful outcome. Purity preserves us in grace. Today preservatives are common chemical additives in most foods. Food manufacturers add them so as to preserve the shelf life of their products and thus make available to the ever-fussy consumer a greater range of food items. Once upon a time there were no artificial preservatives and food variety was seasonal and thus limited. Back then people did survive and, let's admit it, there were fewer health issues such as obesity, diabetes or heart disease. It is a given fact that that some illnesses are diet related.

What's the point, you may be asking? Today, unlike fifty years ago, the media, entertainment and information resources have, beyond all expectations, escalated in providing us with enormous opportunities and options, in addition to temptations. The reality of sin and the 'occasions of sin' are constant in some homes. Apart from TV and DVD's, there is the ever-present internet that promotes pornography in so many subtle and deceitful forms. Technology, like food, is not evil in itself but it does need to be controlled. People add chemical preservatives to ensure the long life of their products; we need to add purity so as to preserve and prepare us for eternal life. God's grace can be diluted, contaminated and even lost.

Reverence the presence within

In the letters of Saint Paul we are reminded that, since our Baptism, we belong to God. "Do you not know that you are God's temple and that God's Spirit dwells in you? If anyone destroys God's temple, God will destroy him. For God's temple is holy, and that temple you are" (1 Corinthians 3:16-17).

What powerful sentiments and great expectations await those who are bearers of divine Grace. As pots carry water, we bear within our earthen 'pots' God's divine life or 'living water'. For that reason alone, we are obliged to cherish that which we have been given and to protect it for ourselves and for the sake of others. When someone is of value we respect that person. If we bear within us God's Grace, how can we not respect ourselves and others? Purity preserves and maintains that respect.

Purity thus conveys a positive affirmation of one's sexuality, one's soul and body with readiness to affirm the value of the person in every situation. A person in possession of the virtue of holy purity is capable of perceiving the mystery of sex in its depth and intimacy, a mystery that provokes reverence, because he reveres the profound relationship it has with God and His creation. Sex belongs in a special manner to God.

Holy purity is a reverent attitude towards sexuality that results in a joyful affirmation of the whole person. This appreciation of holy purity as a *reverent attitude* to sexuality helps one to understand its nature as such, but, I still need to ask myself: what is the best way to exercise this virtue? How is it lived out?

Saint Paul exhorts us to walk by the Spirit and to not gratify the desires of the flesh. For the desires of the flesh are against the Spirit and the desires of the Spirit are against the flesh (cf. Romans 8:8-9; Galatians 5:16-17). Man who lives not by the Spirit lives by the flesh and is bound to the threefold concupiscence to which Saint John refers: lust of the flesh, of the eyes, and the pride of life (cf. 1 John 2:16).

Too many young people have never been taught that we Christians, having been created in the image of God, are His living temples. Therefore we do not profane that which belongs to God, lest we be destroyed ourselves. Another word for destruction would be disintegration. That is the negative consequence of an immoral choice. The positive response requires that we give ample reverence to others, those who are baptized, because they bear divine Grace.

If we want to belong to Christ and grow in holiness we must flee from the threefold concupiscence: "God has not called us for uncleanness, but in holiness. Therefore whosoever disregards this, disregards not man but God, who gives His Spirit to you" (1 Thessalonians 4:7-8). In order to attain perfection in imitation of Christ some people have been called to the single consecrated life.

Righteous Religious

From the very beginning of the Church men and women have set about following Christ and imitating Him through the practice of a life dedicated to God. Many of them, under the inspiration of the Holy Spirit, lived as hermits or founded religious families, which the Church gladly welcomed and approved by her authority. So in accordance with the Divine Plan, a wonderful variety of religious communities emerged so that the Church was equipped for every good work — the building up of the Body of Christ (cf. Ephesians 4:12).

In the early Church one consequence of the religious movement was an attitude of unholy disdain for Marriage. The holy sought perfection in the consecrated state, while others followed the normal path of Marriage which was regarded as second place for those not aspiring towards perfection. One theologian who fought the good fight by defending Marriage as a means to holiness was Saint Augustine. Commonly referred to as the Doctor of Grace because of his treatises and letters on the nature of grace, he asserted that our bodies are grace-filled temples, even for those who are married.

In the midst of many conflicting ideas in the fifth century, Augustine took from the past what was good and merged it with current ideas so as to weld a balanced doctrine on Marriage. When he wrote his classic text *On the Good of Marriage* (399-401) he was forty-six years old and had been a bishop for only four years. Saint Augustine was an amazing scholar and bishop for all that he wrote — remember, in those days there were no laptops!

Concerning the status of Marriage, some exalted it above all other vocations, while others held it in disdain, such as the Manicheans, a sect of which Augustine was once a member before his conversion. They taught that the body was inferior to the mind and even perverse. Augustine's solution to the complicated debate was neither too optimistic nor pessimistic and for that very reason his theological reasoning has endured down through the centuries. Even Pope Pius XI in his classic *Encyclical Letter on Marriage* in 1930, followed his framework of the threefold goods [*bona*] of Marriage: procreation, fidelity and indissolubility.

The heart of the debate focussed on the exact relationship between concupiscence (inordinate desires of the body resulting from original sin) and purity. As Marriage seems to foster bodily concupiscence, many misguided souls dismissed it from being a pure state of life. The Bishop of Hippo resolved this dilemma in the following manner. At the very beginning of *On Marriage and Concupiscence* (418), written to Valerius at Ravenna, Augustine insists that in spite of concupiscence Marriage remains a good vocation. One must distinguish between the goodness of Marriage, which had existed before sin, and concupiscence, which is the result of sin. Surely it is wrong, he asked himself, to condemn Marriage because of carnal desires which come not from Marriage but from sin. The Bishop of Hippo masterfully never condemned Marriage because of pleasure nor praised it solely because of pleasure.

Sexual relations of spouses, said Saint Augustine, with the intention to procreate is a good [*bonum*] of matrimony. But, he adds, if such relations are used solely for pleasure, as in the case of animals, without the intention of procreation, then spouses are impure and dishonest. But are spouses pure if their sexual relations are not in view of procreation? Providing spouses do not oppose procreation, they have the right to relations. Augustine does not object to sterile or elderly couples uniting in love. The conjugal act is a good in itself. However, procreation alone does not make one pure. Couples need to be united to God in faith and then because they cooperate with him in the work of creation they become pure. Once again we note the link here between purity and the virtue of faith.

Clarity of Heaven

In recent years, Pope John Paul II's *Theology of the Body* has added much clarity to this whole debate. We now know that the marital act is not just good, but with the right intention is holy. The vocation to Marriage is a beautiful and holy vocation willed by God and instilled in our nature as creatures created in God's Triune image. God is a Family in Heaven. He wills that we on earth as pilgrims reflect and build up His earthly family in expectation of being members of the royal and eternal family in the Kingdom of God.

Despite such a high appraisal, Marriage is nonetheless temporal, and does not exist in the realm of eternal life. In reply to the Sadducees concerning the resurrection, Jesus said: "For when they rise from the dead, they neither marry nor are given in Marriage ... in heaven" (Mark 12:24). After the general resurrection of the bodies (CCC 997) in the age to come, we "are equal to angels and are sons of God" (Luke 20:36). Be quite clear that there is no Marriage in Heaven. But, wait, in Heaven there is more to ecstasy and loving relationships than wedded bliss. Saint Paul provided us with an insight when he said: "What no eye has seen, nor ear heard, nor the heart of man conceived, what God has prepared for those who love him" (1 Corinthians 2:9).

It is for this reason that the consecrated state is the present sign of that spiritual communion awaiting all who are justified in the Lord. Priests and nuns are now what we all shall be in eternity with God. Only then will there be perfect bodily union with the soul and a certain divinisation of the person so that we are able to see God face-to-face (cf. Revelation 22:4). The latter endowment in itself renders a communion with God and the saints that will surpass all expectations and will be the definitive fulfilment of the nuptial meaning of the body — a meaning that is not yet realised in Marriage.

Such an elevation of the consecrated state does not diminish the sanctity of marriage. Instead, it manifests the mutual complementarity between the two vocations. Yet it ought to be noted that the consecrated state is more sacred and perfect because it pursues as a direct end God and the perfection of charity while marriage pursues mutual self-giving love between the spouses as its formal object.

Consecrated vocation

The consecrated state is not a natural but a *supernatural* vocation. Not all are now called to the consecrated state that awaits everyone in eternity; so one cannot be commanded or coerced to pursue this vocation. It is a calling from the Lord: "and there are eunuchs, who have made themselves eunuchs for the sake of the kingdom of heaven. He who is able to receive this, let him receive it" (Matthew 19:12). From the beginning God has called some, such as Saint Paul, to serve Him, "to please the Lord" (1 Corinthians 7:32).

Even in the Old Testament, God Himself *consecrated* persons or objects by imparting His holiness in some way to them. God inwardly sanctified objects in the sense that He took possession of them and set them apart for His direct service. The 'sacred' objects were intended for the worship of the Lord, and thus could only be used in the temple and during worship, and not for what was profane (meaning: in front of the temple or outside of it). This sacredness was attributed to things that could not be touched by profane hands, as, for example, the Ark of the Covenant, the cups of the Temple in Jerusalem that were profaned by King Belteshazzar (Daniel 5:1-31) and Antiochus Epiphanes (1 Maccabees 1:22).

The consecrated state of persons employs the evangelical counsels or vows of poverty, chastity and obedience for the growth of the Church's holiness (cf. CCC 915). Different religious families have come into existence in which spiritual resources are multiplied for the progress in holiness of their members and for the good of the entire Body of Christ (CCC 918).

Despite such a great variety of gifts, all those called by God to the practice of the evangelical counsels follow in a special way Christ who was chaste and poor. Driven by the love with which the Holy Spirit floods their hearts (cf. Romans 5:5) they live more and more for Christ and for His body which is the Church (cf. Colossians 1:24). The more fervently, then, they are joined to Christ by this total lifelong gift of themselves, the richer the life of the Church becomes and the more lively and successful its apostolate. In turn this explains why when the number of religious has dwindled the Church's work of evangelization has become so marginal.

Celibate Clergy

In the early Church there were always men and women who, contrary to the Jewish norms, literally followed the example of Christ and lived a celibate life. It should not be regarded as remarkable that those called to the clerical state, to act *in persona Christi* (in the person of Christ), followed the celibate state for the sake of the Lord. In recent years theologians such as Roman Cholij, Stefan Heid and Christian Cochini S.J., have provided insights into the clerical state of the early Church. In the beginning, clerics came from both the single lifestyle and those who were married but the latter, with their wives permission, embraced the clerical life in a celibate manner. In both cases the obligatory clerical norm of perfect continence, *lex continentiae* was taken for granted.

Over time, for practical reasons, and more than likely on account of the occasional lapse of those who were married, and due to the abundance of single candidates, those eligible for the Priesthood were selected from only the unmarried. Note that there is no record anywhere of a cleric once ordained who was given permission to marry. Never in the history of the Church, both East and West, has this norm varied.

What makes the situation even more vexing is when the media, being biased against Christian sexual norms, assert that priests should be allowed to marry. 'How dare the Church impose this antiquated law on men,' they claim. 'Besides with our present shortage of priests so many of those who had left could return to active ministry, if only the Church relaxed her celibacy law.' In reply, be convinced and try to convince shallow-minded souls that sacramental norms are based on Scripture and Sacred Tradition that clearly forbid priests to marry. That means that never has a man once ordained to Holy Orders been allowed to marry and function as a priest. Even among the Orthodox Churches where there are married clergy, one marries first and then one is ordained to serve, not vice-versa. Records indicate that, from the fourth century, men who were called to the Priesthood were required to adopt celibate lives. It was only in the East after the Council of Trullo in the seventh century — of which specific matters were not approved by the Church — that priests were permitted to remain married with conjugal rights after ordination. Note, however, that bishops were only ever chosen from among the celibate clergy.

Married Priests

Married clergy do exist, however, when the rare situation arises of a non-Catholic married clergyman, such as an Anglican minister, converting to the Catholic faith and requesting permission to be ordained a Catholic priest. In such cases, the Holy See examines the case and once a period of time has transpired after reception into full communion with the

Catholic Church and provided he has satisfied academic and personal requirements, he may receive Holy Orders. Normally such procedures require five or so years. Once again, the principle is maintained that Marriage precedes ordination. In these rare cases, the pastoral placement is given much consideration, to protect family life.

On another note, time has proven that the benefits of celibacy far outweigh any supposed flaws. It is at the same time a sign and a stimulus to pastoral charity and a special source of spiritual fruitfulness for the sake of the flock commended to them. Saint Peter said to the Lord: "Lo, we have left all things and have followed you." And He said to them: "Truly, I say to you, there is no man who has left home or *wife* or brothers or parents or children, for the sake of the kingdom of God, who will not receive manifold in this time, and in the age to come eternal life" (Luke 18:28-30).

Through virginity or celibacy observed for the Kingdom of Heaven, priests are consecrated to Christ for the sake of the mission. They adhere to him more easily with an undivided heart, they dedicate themselves more freely to him and to the service of God and his faithful as a spiritual father, possessing a paternity in Christ. Notice how St John in his letter calls his converts his own children, and St Paul in his letter to the Galatians said, *"You are my children and I was in labour with you over and over again until you took the shape of Christ"* (Galations 4:19).

Likewise, St Paul – when he wrote to Philemon about the runaway slave – said, *"I am appealing to you for my child, Onesimus, whose father I have become during my imprisonment"* (Philemon 1:10). St Peter knew only too well of this spiritual progeny because in his first letter he wrote, *"Your new birth was not from any mortal seed but from the everlasting word of the living and eternal God."* (1 Peter 1:23).

This paternity in Christ was foretold by the prophet Isaiah: *"Sing aloud oh barren woman who never bore a child. Break into cries of joy you who have never been in labour. For you shall have more sons that she who lives in wedlock"* (Isaiah 54:1).

Indeed, celibacy has a many-faceted suitability for the Priesthood. For the whole priestly mission is dedicated to the service of a new humanity which Christ, the Victor over death, has raised up through His Spirit in the world and which has its origin "not of blood, nor of the will of the flesh, nor of the will of man but of God" (Jn 1:13).

Conclusion

Whatever our vocation, be it to the consecrated life or Marriage, we are called to love. It is the primordial vocation of each and every human person. When we love in a self-giving manner in this life, we are being moulded in the 'art of love' so as to enter eternal life with the God of love (1 John 4:16). In each case, purity purifies our love, it refines it so that the manner in which we love is more selfless and therefore more holy, bringing us ever closer to the eternal perfection of the life to come.

Pure Attraction

www.ingramcontent.com/pod-product-compliance
Ingram Content Group UK Ltd.
Pitfield, Milton Keynes, MK11 3LW, UK
UKHW020642070726
13597UKWH00018B/120